# 25 MINI-PLAYS
# WORLD HISTORY

## SCHOLASTIC
## PROFESSIONAL BOOKS

New York • Toronto • London • Auckland • Sydney
Mexico City • New Delhi • Hong Kong

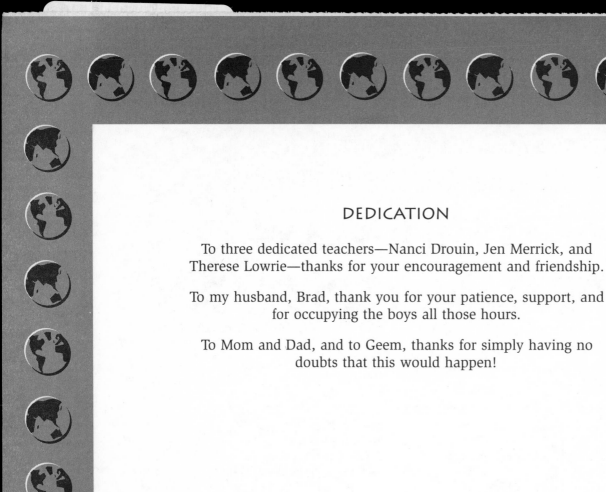

## DEDICATION

To three dedicated teachers—Nanci Drouin, Jen Merrick, and
Therese Lowrie—thanks for your encouragement and friendship.

To my husband, Brad, thank you for your patience, support, and
for occupying the boys all those hours.

To Mom and Dad, and to Geem, thanks for simply having no
doubts that this would happen!

Written by Erin Fry
Edited by Sarah Glasscock

Cover design by Jaime Lucero
Interior design by Melinda Belter
Cover art and interior illustrations by Mona Mark

ISBN 0-439-14009-9

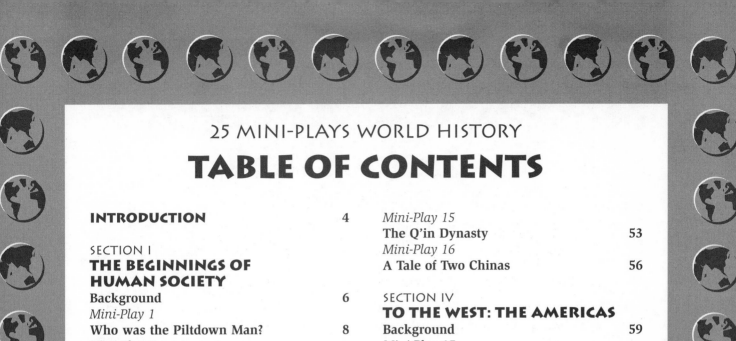

# 25 MINI-PLAYS WORLD HISTORY
# TABLE OF CONTENTS

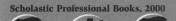

# INTRODUCTION

STUDYING ANCIENT HISTORY CAN BE A DAUNTING TASK FOR MANY MIDDLE school students who struggle to comprehend events in distant times and foreign places. How can teachers help students enjoy this history and make connections to their own lives—and still meet curricular objectives?

These teacher-developed mini-plays connect students with the drama of history and provide a focused link to ancient world history lesson objectives. The mini-plays present subject matter in a familiar, exciting format that features historical figures as real people who interacted with one another in very different settings from ours. The scripts are short, so students do not feel overwhelmed by lengthy dialogue or numerous details. They are meant to be used in conjunction with and to expand upon the content and ideas presented in textbooks, trade books, and other curricular materials.

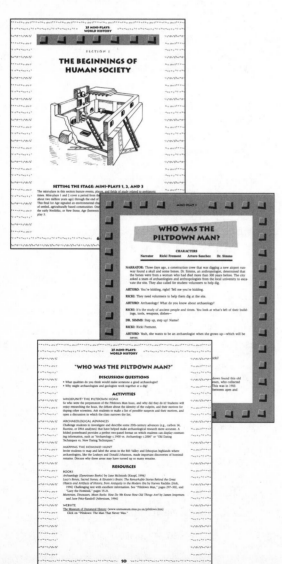

*25 Mini-Plays: World History* is divided into the following sections:
I. The Beginnings of Human Society;
II. The Cradle of Civilization and Beyond;
III. To the East: India and China;
IV. To the West: The Americas; V. Greece; and VI. Rome. The areas of study and student activities in this book correspond with Eras 1, 2, and 3 of the National World History Standards developed by the National Center for History in the Schools.

Each section opens with historical background that provides details about the featured events and characters. And every mini-play is followed by discussion questions, engaging activities, and literature and Internet links to encourage further investigation with primary and secondary resources. Feel free to adjust the activities to meet the needs and interests of your students.

Also included in this resource are tips on ways to make the most of mini-plays in your classroom. The introduction presents helpful suggestions for lesson and time-management planning with mini-plays. The appendix offers additional student resources on acting and playwriting to be used with the mini-plays.

# FITTING MINI-PLAYS INTO YOUR LESSONS

**PREFACE TO A LESSON:**
When you present a mini-play prior to teaching a lesson, you invite active student participation in a quick overview of the historical material. Whether you allow your student actors time to rehearse or simply conduct a quick read-through, mini-plays offer a more engaging and motivating format than do traditional introductory formats, such as textbook passages or lecture notes.

**REVIEW OF A LESSON:**
Working with a mini-play after a lesson helps students remember the lesson and connect the mini-play to the larger history curriculum. Students can use note-taking strategies, such as underlining key words and jotting notes in the script margins, to help them remember and respond to important information.

**JIGSAW:**
To cover a broad span of historical material quickly, you may want to divide your class into groups and assign each group a different script related to the time period or civilization that you are teaching. Each group can then practice and perform its mini-play for the entire class. Presenting a chronological sequence of mini-plays at once offers an overview of different topics you plan to cover in a given unit.

# ALLOWING TIME FOR MINI-PLAYS

**THE TEN MINUTE METHOD:**
Simply hand each student a copy of the mini-play, select students for the different parts, and then conduct a read-through without much preparation. Most parts are short, so even struggling readers will find the scripts accessible and volunteer to participate in this activity. Feel free to involve more students in the drama by inviting several students to read the same part chorally. The read-through will help strengthen oral reading skills in a purposeful, nonthreatening group format.

**THE PRACTICE MAKES PERFECT METHOD:**
You may sometimes want to offer the scripts to a handful of selected students in advance, assign roles, and encourage them to practice their parts at home or as a small group while the rest of the class works on another task. This strategy works especially well for readers who need extra time to feel comfortable with material that they will read aloud. It also allows students time to act out their lines, something that takes practice to do well. Students may especially enjoy getting into the act if you encourage them to ad-lib lines and create costumes and props.

**THE LET'S ALL TRY IT METHOD:**
Occasionally, you and your students may enjoy preparing contrasting versions of the same scene in history. In this case, provide each member of the class with a copy of the same script, divide the class into groups (according to the cast size), and let each group rehearse the script. Then schedule each group to take its turn performing the skit in front of the class. The class should note differences and similarities among the presentations. In this way, everyone participates in the mini-plays. Furthermore, students become well versed with and entertain different perspectives on the featured material.

## SECTION I

# THE BEGINNINGS OF HUMAN SOCIETY

## SETTING THE STAGE: MINI-PLAYS 1, 2, AND 3

The mini-plays in this section feature events, places, and fields of study related to prehistoric times. Mini-plays 1 and 2 cover a period from the Paleolithic, or Old Stone, Age (beginning about two million years ago) through the end of the last Ice Age (ending about 11,000 BC). This final Ice Age signaled an environmental change that encouraged the growth and spread of settled, agriculturally based communities. One of the first known cities to develop during the early Neolithic, or New Stone, Age (between c. 8000 BC and 3000 BC) is the topic of mini-play 3.

# BACKGROUND

**"Who was the Piltdown Man?"** opens this unit with an introduction to archaeology. The characters refer to a sensational 1908 "discovery" in which skull, jaw, and teeth fragments from a site in Piltdown, England, were falsely attributed to the Pleistocene era. However, a half century later, scientists proved that the Piltdown remains were no more than a miscellaneous collection of human, ape, and other animal fossils doctored to look authentic. This mini-play highlights the growth of scientific methods involved in archaeology, and how experts from a variety of fields can work together to solve problems.

Many anthropologists believe that our species evolved from earlier hominids between 400,000 and 300,000 BC. Homo sapiens ("thinking man") left behind evidence of his toolmaking abilities, such as flint for making stone tools, stone foundations from temporary shelters, and contemporary animal bones. Archaeologists have studied such artifacts discovered at a temporary settlement at Terra Amata in southern France dating to 250,000 BC. **"Around the Fire at Terra Amata"** re-creates a scene from this era.

In the 1950s, at the bottom of a hill built up over 800 years of urban growth, one of the first cities of the Neolithic Age was discovered. The original inhabitants of this site in present-day Turkey built an impressive network of rectangular, adjoining houses; courtyards; and shrines that formed a solid, impenetrable wall of defense around the city. The protagonists in **"Adventure in Çatal Hüyük"** discover the unique way these city dwellers moved from one building to the next—by climbing through hatches on rooftops, walking across roofs, and scaling ladders to reach different levels. People in this settled community not only refined toolmaking but also advanced agriculture and social organization. Notably, women played a major role in all aspects of society at Çatal Hüyük—social, economic, political, and religious.

# WHO WAS THE PILTDOWN MAN?

## CHARACTERS

**Narrator**    **Ricki Fremont**    **Arturo Sanchez**    **Dr. Simms**

**NARRATOR:** Three days ago, a construction crew that was digging a new airport runway found a skull and some bones. Dr. Simms, an anthropologist, determined that the bones were from a woman who had died more than 300 years before. The city asked a team of archaeologists and anthropologists from the local university to excavate the site. They also called for student volunteers to help dig.

**ARTURO:** You're kidding, right? Tell me you're kidding.

**RICKI:** They need volunteers to help them dig at the site.

**ARTURO:** Archaeology! What do you know about archaeology?

**RICKI:** It's the study of ancient people and times. You look at what's left of their buildings, tools, weapons, dishes—

**DR. SIMMS:** Step up, step up! Name?

**RICKI:** Ricki Fremont.

**ARTURO:** Yeah, she wants to be an archaeologist when she grows up—which will be never.

**DR. SIMMS:** Really? Why?

**ARTURO:** Well, she has these dreams that'll never come true.

**DR. SIMMS:** Why do you want to become an archaeologist, Ricki?

**RICKI:** The Piltdown Man.

**ARTURO:** Hey, is that like the Pillsbury Dough—

**RICKI:** No. Some workers near a village in England called Piltdown found this old brown skull one day. They took it to a man named Mr. Dawson, who collected fossils. He dug around some more and found more bones. This was in 1910. Some scientists decided the bones were the "missing link" between apes and humans, and they named him *Eoanthropus dawsoni*.

**DR. SIMMS:** Excellent, Ricki.

**ARTURO:** *Dawsoni?* Hey, if I dig around and find something, can I name it after me? *Sanchezi?* That sounds pretty good.

**RICKI:** The scientists were wrong. The Piltdown Man wasn't even a man at all! Everybody found out later that the skull was from an orangutan. The bones weren't even that old.

**DR. SIMMS:** That's right. It wasn't until 1950, after the fluorine dating technique had been invented, that the hoax was discovered.

**ARTURO:** "The fluorine dating technique"? That sounds like something my sister uses on Saturday night.

**DR. SIMMS:** The bones had been stained and doctored to make them look older, and the test was able to show that.

**ARTURO:** So somebody messed with some bones and made up a story about them. What's the big deal?

**RICKI:** Because real bones were being found in other places, like Africa, and nobody could make them fit in with the Piltdown Man. The Piltdown Man threw everybody off the track for a while. That's why I want to be an archaeologist. I want to make sure we don't get thrown off the track again.

**ARTURO:** I'm good at that, getting thrown off the track.

**DR. SIMMS:** How are you at digging carefully and patiently?

**ARTURO:** Can I keep any cool-looking rocks I find? I like to collect rocks.

**DR. SIMMS:** Afraid not. Our geologists are using the rocks to tell us about what the environment was like more than 300 years ago.

**ARTURO:** You can tell all that from rocks? Hey, maybe I'm geologist material.

**DR. SIMMS:** You're both hired. Here are your tools. Remember—

**RICKI AND ARTURO:** Dig carefully and patiently.

**ARTURO:** And don't slip any rocks into your backpack.

# "WHO WAS THE PILTDOWN MAN?"

## DISCUSSION QUESTIONS

• What qualities do you think would make someone a good archaeologist?
• Why might archaeologists and geologists work together at a dig?

## ACTIVITIES

### WHODUNIT? THE PILTDOWN HOAX

So who were the perpetrators of the Piltdown Man hoax, and why did they do it? Students will enjoy researching the hoax, the debate about the identity of the culprits, and their motives for duping other scientists. Ask students to make a list of possible suspects and their motives, and open a discussion in which the class narrows the list.

### ARCHAEOLOGICAL ADVANCES

Challenge students to investigate and describe some 20th-century advances (e.g., carbon 14, fluorine, or DNA analyses) that have helped make archaeological research more accurate. A folded posterboard provides a perfect two-panel format on which students can display contrasting information, such as "Archaeology c.1900 vs. Archaeology c.2000" or "Old Dating Techniques vs. New Dating Techniques."

### MAPPING THE HOMINID HUNT

Invite students to map and label the areas in the Rift Valley and Ethiopian highlands where archaeologists, like the Leakeys and Donald Johanson, made important discoveries of hominid remains. Discuss why these areas may have turned up so many remains.

## RESOURCES

### BOOKS

*Archaeology (Eyewitness Books)* by Jane McIntosh (Knopf, 1994)

*Lucy's Bones, Sacred Stones, & Einstein's Brain: The Remarkable Stories Behind the Great Objects and Artifacts of History, from Antiquity to the Modern Era* by Harvey Rachlin (Holt, 1996) Challenging text with excellent information. See "Piltdown Man," pages 297–302, and "Lucy the Hominid," pages 15-21.

*Mummies, Dinosaurs, Moon Rocks: How Do We Know How Old Things Are?* by James Jespersen and Jane Fritz-Randolf (Athenium, 1996)

### WEBSITE

The Museum of Unnatural History (www.unmuseum.mus.pa.us/piltdown.htm)
Click on "Piltdown: The Man That Never Was."

# AROUND THE FIRE AT TERRA AMATA

### CHARACTERS

Narrator    Bandu (a storyteller)
Geon (leader of group)    Man    Sark (a toolmaker)    Woman

**NARRATOR:** The time is 3,000 years ago, on the shores of the Mediterranean Sea. A group of about 20 people are gathered around a campfire inside a small hut made of sticks and stones, which is their only protection against the outdoors. This is Terra Amata, a camp the group sets up every spring. Bandu, the clan's storyteller, begins to tell a story.

**BANDU:** *(As if telling a story)* The hunter had magical powers and so decided to transform himself into a rabbit. As a rabbit, he could get very close to the other rabbits without startling them and causing them to run off. In this way, he could kill his prey easily and quickly.

**GEON:** That was a wonderful tale, Bandu, one of my favorites. But I think it's time for us to sleep now. Tomorrow, the men will hunt for more meat, and the women will gather berries.

**MAN:** If we bring back any new skins, we'll need new flaying knives. Most of our knives are chipped or dull.

**GEON:** Sark, you'll have to start on the new knives in the morning. Do you have enough flint for the task?

**SARK:** I have enough right now to make two more knives to flay animal skins and one borer to help the women with the sewing. Are we planning to follow the herd of deer we saw come near early this morning?

**GEON:** The deer are our best chance for meat.

**WOMAN:** We found a fig tree near the spring. We'll gather some figs tomorrow morning when we go for water. Then we'll start weaving the baskets for the children to carry.

**GEON:** Agreed. It's still cold; we'll keep the fire burning tonight.

**NARRATOR:** The men, women, and children all find an animal fur for warmth and a place to sleep in the small hut. It's a tight squeeze, but the group is used to cramped quarters. The small space helps them stay warm and get the sleep they need. Various animal bones scattered around show what they've eaten today—birds, turtles, rabbits, and fish. Tomorrow, if they are lucky, they will feast on deer, pigs, or even elephants.

Remnants of this hut remained in southern France until 1965, when it was destroyed to make room for some buildings and a parking lot.

# "AROUND THE FIRE AT TERRA AMATA"

## DISCUSSION QUESTIONS

- Sometimes people want to destroy historical sites like Terra Amata because modern buildings or roads need to be built. What criteria would you set to determine whether a site is worth keeping? Who should decide?
- What kinds of remains of life at Terra Amata would *not* have been preserved after thousands of years? How does this affect our understanding of history?

## ACTIVITIES

### IT'S CRAMPED IN HERE!

Before you and your class read this play, tape out an area on the floor that would approximate the size of the Terra Amata hut (20 to 25 feet long by about 10 to 15 feet wide). Conduct the day's lesson (or part of it!) in these cramped quarters with all the students and their materials inside the taped boundaries. Debrief students by asking how uncomfortable they were, what the hardships might have been for these early humans, and what activities would have been difficult in such a crowded living space.

### DAILY LIFE AT TERRA AMATA

Challenge students to investigate archaeological evidence found at Terra Amata and write a brief description of a day in the life of a hunter or gatherer camped there. Then invite students to compare their descriptions in pairs or small groups. Have them consider the way their point of view and limited archaeological evidence might account for the differences in descriptions. Students may evaluate what parts of their descriptions were best supported by historical evidence. Ask how this description differs from a fictional account.

### A CLASS DIG!

Conduct an archaeological hunt through . . . the garbage! Pose the question: *What evidence of your community and lifestyle might survive a thousand years from now?* Have students list or collect materials found in garbage and recycling bins and determine whether these items could be artifacts. Then challenge students to take their entire lists and classify evidence into categories such as tools, shelter, clothing, trade, religion, and others the class may generate. Discuss which categories have the least amount of evidence available and which have the most. How much of this evidence do students think will be available a millennium from today and how might this affect research about our civilization?

## RESOURCES

### BOOKS

*An Ice Age Hunter (Everyday Life* series*)* by Giovanni Caselli (Peter Bedrick Books, 1992)
*Early Humans (Eyewitness Books)* edited by Philip Wilkinson (Knopf, 1989)

### WEBSITE

<u>Stone Age Habitats</u> (www.personal.psu.edu/users/w/x/wxk116/)
    The site includes two drawings of huts at Terra Amata and reconstructions of other
    Paleolithic campsites.

# ADVENTURE IN ÇATAL HÜYÜK

## CHARACTERS

**Narrator    Jackie    Bobby    Dr. Digg    Ms. Boerang**

**NARRATOR:** Jackie and Bobby doze in their world history class while their teacher, Ms. Boerang, talks about the ancient city of Çatal Hüyük (*chuh-TUL hoo-YOOK*) in Turkey. Jackie is snoring softly. Bobby's mouth is open. But moments later, both students wake up in a strange city.

**JACKIE:** Whoa—where are we, Bobby?

**BOBBY:** Oh, man, it looks like some alien planet out of a *Star Wars* movie. Do you think we time-warped to another planet?

**JACKIE:** This is a totally weird place. Look, none of the buildings have doors.

**BOBBY:** That dude's climbing a ladder to get to the roof. Let's follow him.

**NARRATOR:** After Jackie and Bobby climb the ladder, they find themselves on a very flat roof. They can see many people climbing in and out of holes in the roofs and using ladders to get from one rooftop to another since the roofs are at different levels. A large group of people are entering one particular hole.

**BOBBY:** What do you think is going on over there?

**JACKIE:** I don't know. Let's check it out. Maybe it's a party or something.

**BOBBY:** Awesome! Party on.

**NARRATOR:** Jackie and Bobby travel across the roofs until they reach the hole that everyone had been climbing in and out of. Smoke pours out of the hole.

**JACKIE:** Do you think this is a chimney, Bobby?

**BOBBY:** Cool! It's like we're Santa Claus or something!

**NARRATOR:** Jackie and Bobby don't realize that in Çatal Hüyük, the holes, used as "doors" to homes, also serve as chimneys where smoke from the fires below can escape to the outside. Gasping and choking from the smoke, Jackie and Bobby climb into the hole and down to a dark room below.

**JACKIE:** This is an awfully small house—only two rooms.

**BOBBY:** Yeah, and look—they don't even have furniture. Just those benches built into the walls.

**JACKIE:** Everyone here looks so sad. I don't think this is a party after all.

**BOBBY:** That woman lying on the bench next to you? Does she look . . . does she look dead to you?

**NARRATOR:** Suddenly, a tall man appears out of nowhere.

**BOBBY:** Whoa, dude! Who are you?

**DR. DIGG:** Dr. Digg, archaeologist, sent into your dream to explain what's going on since you two obviously don't listen in class.

**JACKIE:** So, anyway, Dr. D., why does that woman over there look dead?

**DR. DIGG:** Because she is. This is a funeral. She'll be buried under that platform. In this culture, they bury their dead relatives in their homes.

**BOBBY:** I don't think so. That's totally gross. I'm getting out of here.

**NARRATOR:** Bobby and Jackie hurry up the ladder to the roof. Dr. Digg magically appears beside them again.

**DR. DIGG:** Did you notice the paintings on the wall? The room you were in was the family shrine, a place of worship. There are many shrines here; in fact, it's become the religious center of the valley. Çatal Hüyük has become quite self-sufficient. These people grow enough food to feed themselves; they don't have to depend on others for their survival.

**JACKIE:** Maybe so, but somebody should clue them in about cemeteries.

**DR. DIGG:** The people here do many things, since not everyone has to hunt and farm. They make needles, beads, and fishhooks. They weave cloth, make baskets, and do leather work. I'd love to show you around more, but it's time to . . .

**MS. BOERANG:** . . . close your books and take out a pen for today's quiz.

**JACKIE AND BOBBY:** *(Sleepily)* Huh? What's going on?

**MS. BOERANG:** Sit up, please. I hope you two were paying attention.

**NARRATOR:** Jackie and Bobby wake up in Ms. Boerang's classroom with a pop quiz in front of them. Glancing at the first question, both are surprised to discover that they actually know the answer. Grinning at each other, they eagerly pick up their pens and finish the quiz before anybody else in the class.

Scholastic Professional Books, 2000

# "ADVENTURE IN ÇATAL HÜYÜK"

## DISCUSSION QUESTIONS

- How does Çatal Hüyük compare with the early hunting and gathering communities of the Ice Age, such as the one at Terra Amata?
- How did the community of Çatal Hüyük solve problems of a large, permanent population?

## ACTIVITIES

### CONSTRUCTION SITE, C. 6000 BC

Invite students to study the architectural layout of houses in Çatal Hüyük. In pairs or small groups, they may work collaboratively to construct a model of a building or group of buildings. Students should be able to describe the materials that would have been used in the construction and the functions of different rooms.

### EARLY HUMANS' WALL STREET: THE NECESSITY OF TRADING

After exploring life in Çatal Hüyük, set up a mini Wall Street in your classroom to help students understand how trading began. Break the class into small groups of students and provide each group with different amounts of materials needed to make a simple object, like a paper snowman. For example, one group receives only white circles; another receives glue; a third receives paper carrot noses, and so on. Make sure some groups have a surplus of supplies while others have a scarcity. Then invite groups to trade with one another and compete to be the first group to make a complete snowman. This activity lends itself to a discussion about renewable resources (like glue) versus nonrenewable resources (like paper) and how scarcities and surpluses dictate the value of materials and the final product.

### TOOLMAKING AT ÇATAL HÜYÜK

Encourage students to analyze illustrations of various tools crafted by the self-sufficient city dwellers at Çatal Hüyük. They may design a pamphlet that pictures and describes the uses of these tools. The pamphlets should explain how these objects affected daily life in Çatal Hüyük.

## RESOURCES

### BOOKS

*The First Civilizations (History of Everyday Things)* by Giovanni Caselli (Peter Bedrick, 1998)
*The Rise of Cities (Timeframe)* by TimeLife editors (TimeLife, 1991)

### WEBSITE

21St C Art, CE-BC, A Context by Jan Haag, Heinrich Klotz, and Jeffrey Shaw
   (http://students.washington.edu/jhaag/osch.htm)
   This site offers images of early printed cloth designs and fascinating virtual reconstructions of interior spaces of Çatal Hüyük.

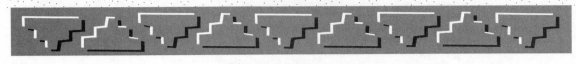

# SECTION II

# THE CRADLE OF CIVILIZATION AND BEYOND:
# MESOPOTAMIA, EGYPT, KUSH, AND THE MIDDLE EAST

## SETTING THE STAGE: MINI-PLAYS 4, 5, 6, 7, 8, 9, AND 10

The mini-plays in this section introduce students to rulers, notable figures, and other voices from two of the first major riverside civilizations: the Fertile Crescent of the Middle East and the Nile River valley of Egypt. The plays also highlight major changes in the political, social, and economic lives of different peoples in these areas and mark the rise of monotheism as a major religious institution.

## BACKGROUND

During the Neolithic Age, the fertile soil on the sunny plains between the Tigris and Euphrates encouraged nomadic herders from present-day Iran and Armenia to settle and begin to farm in Mesopotamia (now Iraq). By 3200 BC, agricultural settlements and river trade had expanded greatly and required central political organization to ensure stability, order, and economic diversity. In **"Humans and Gods in Mesopotamia,"** students gain an understanding of the early efforts to organize a theocratic government in the region's city-states and the role of a polytheistic religion in everyday life.

As the power of kings and priests grew, so the power of the individual diminished. Accompanying this shift in power was a stark social stratification, with rulers at the top of the order and unskilled laborers, farmers, and slaves at the bottom. By 2350 BC the move toward central control was complete and the city-states united under a single emperor, Sargon. **"Sargon's Rule and Hammurabi's Code"** features the governing strategies of Sargon the Great and the legal accomplishments of a later ruler from Babylonia, Hammurabi (c. 1786–1686 BC).

Like their Mesopotamian neighbors, the people of ancient Egypt depended heavily on the water source closest to them, the Nile River. In about 2700 BC, a heavily centralized government formed under a king, later called "pharaoh," who was considered to be a god with divine powers and wisdom. **"Planning a Pyramid"** underscores the importance of the Nile to Egypt's survival, the great responsibility King Zoser (c. 2630–11 BC) assumed for the well-being of his people, and the important role religion played in daily life.

**"Hatshepsut and Thutmose III"** contrasts the leadership of two important pharaohs from the New Kingdom: Hatshepsut (c. 1490–68 BC), the only female pharaoh in Egypt's history, and her equally ambitious stepson, Thutmose III (d. 1438). Hatshepsut focused on building the strength of the existing empire through increased trade and new building projects, while Thutmose III strove to expand the empire through military conquests.

Powerful Egypt dominated trade with and heavily influenced the cultural development of neighboring peoples, like the Kush in Nubia. But as the mighty kingdom weakened, the tables turned. In 725 BC, the Kush conquered Egypt and controlled the region for a century until the iron-wielding Assyrians invaded. Pushed out of Egypt, the Kush set up a new capital farther down the Nile in Meroë, where agriculture, trade, and ironworking began to thrive. **"Meroë's Warrior Queen"** traces this resilient African civilization to the peak of its power in the 2nd and 1st centuries BC. The script highlights the unusual political organization, with Kush matriarchs, called *candake* by the Romans, as key political leaders.

The ninth mini-play spotlights a relatively small cultural group, the Hebrews, who made a big impact on monotheistic religion in the ancient world. Originally herders from Mesopotamia, the Hebrews escaped famine in their homeland, Canaan, by migrating to Egypt. Egyptian pharaohs—suspicious of Hebrew religious beliefs and in need of cheap labor for their elaborate building projects—enslaved the Hebrews. **"Into Israel,"** set in 1290 BC, illustrates the strong leadership of one semi-legendary Hebrew leader, Moses, who negotiated with the pharaoh, led his people on an exodus back to Canaan, and handed down a set of high moral standards known as the Ten Commandments.

The center of power shifted in the Mesopotamian region many times between the first and second millennium. Despite many military attempts, only the Assyrian Empire (c. 700–612 BC) and the Persian Empire (c. 547–331 BC) successfully united the diverse groups in the areas of present-day North Africa and the Middle East. **"The Persian Empire"** features the unique leadership of the first Persian leader, Cyrus the Great (c. 580–29 BC), and one of his predecessors, Darius I (c. 521–486). These leaders built upon the Assyrian model of a strong central intelligence but departed from the Assyrians' brutal tactics of oppression, instead promoting unity and prosperity. Cyrus the Great and Darius I allowed religious freedom and even chose officials from among local populations in the territories they had conquered. The many distinct cultures represented by this empire contributed to a wealth of advancements during this time.

# HUMANS AND GODS IN MESOPOTAMIA

## CHARACTERS

Narrator 1    Priest    Narrator 2    An (a god)
Enlil (a god)    Enki (a god)    Ninhursag (a goddess)    King

**NARRATOR 1:** In the year 3000 BC, priests ruled the city-states that made up Mesopotamia. The priest was in charge of running the irrigation systems, monitoring the grain stored in the temples, collecting taxes, and making sacrifices to please the gods. The priest—

*(Interrupting Narrator 1, the Priest enters.)*

**PRIEST:** Ah, look at my beautiful temple. It's the most impressive building in the city. I, and I alone, control Sumer and all of its people. Nothing, and no one, can ever take away the power the gods have given me!

**NARRATOR 2:** Sumer was one of the city-states in Mesopotamia. Like people in the other city-states, the Sumerians practiced polytheism—they worshipped many gods and goddesses. They believed that the gods and goddesses controlled everything— droughts, disease, floods, and warfare. The Sumerians—

*(Interrupting, An enters and stands in front of Narrator 2.)*

**AN:** I am An, ruler of the sky, the father of *all* the gods. I—

*(Interrupting, Enlil enters and stands in front of An.)*

**ENLIL:** I am Enlil, the god of air and wind. I kicked out An and became the supreme god. All Sumerians pray to me in times of crisis. They elect a "big man" who guides them into a large field and leads them in prayers to me. When the crisis ends, this big man steps down and returns to his normal life again.

**NARRATOR 1:** But once, a big man refused to step down. That's how Sumerians came to have kings to lead them as well as priests.

**NARRATOR 2:** Nomads, herders from the mountains, invaded the city-states to steal grain and other wealth. They had to compete with the people in the city-states for the precious resources of land and water. The high walls surrounding the city-states didn't stop the invasion of the nomads. Sumer needed a strong military leader. That leader became king. The king—

Scholastic Professional Books, 2000

*(Interrupting, Enki enters and stands in front of Narrator 2.)*

**ENKI:** I am Enki. I rule the waters, including all the lakes, rivers, and seas. The people of Sumer pray to *me* to help them with their trading ventures. Trade is important to a civilization. Trade makes a civilization strong and diverse. Ideas are exchanged, goods are exchanged, language is—

*(Interrupting, Ninhursag enters and stands in front of Enki.)*

**NINHURSAG:** Allow me to introduce myself. I am Ninhursag, the mother goddess. There are other, lesser gods and goddesses—3,000 of them. There's Nanna, the moon god, there's a sun god, a love god, and even a mud-brick god. But I am the mother goddess.

**PRIEST:** Did she say Nanna? I pray to the moon goddess Nanna. She is incredibly powerful. She can do the most evil deeds, and yet she can also give us good crops. We must always strive to please Nanna.

**KING:** While the priest prays to Nanna and tries to please her, I manage the irrigation system, control the grain stored in the temples, and am chief judge.

**PRIEST:** Yes, but I still take care of the temples and make sacrifices to the gods.

**NARRATOR 1:** Of course you do. You're still a very powerful ruler, but now you share the power with the king.

**AN:** Yes, but both Priest and King are appointed by the gods and goddesses. They serve *our* will.

**NINHURSAG:** Everyone in Sumer, rich or poor, serves us in some way. They create art to honor us. We play an important part in their everyday lives.

**NARRATOR 2:** The Sumerians did believe that their kings and priests were chosen by the gods and goddesses, who gave those rulers the power to rule as they saw fit. Both rulers were examples of how important religion was to the people of these early city-states.

*(Interrupting, An steps in front of Narrator 2.)*

**AN:** Enlil may have kicked me out, but it's only temporary.

# "HUMANS AND GODS IN MESOPOTAMIA"

## DISCUSSION QUESTIONS

• Name one benefit and one drawback of early Sumerian leadership under two "divinely appointed" powers: a priest and a king. Why might this structure not have lasted?

• How would you describe the role religion played in the life of a Sumerian citizen? How would a priest justify his high social position?

## ACTIVITIES

### CHARTING CIVILIZATION

What makes a civilization different from other social groups? As a class, develop criteria for the term "civilization." With input from students, design a large chart that outlines the ways Mesopotamian civilization meets these criteria. Encourage students to add sections to the chart for comparison and contrast as they study other early civilizations, such as the Nile, Indus Valley, and Yellow River Valley.

### DAILY PLANNER, SUMER-STYLE

Have pairs of students work together as research teams: one partner gathers information on Sumerian gods and goddesses while the other researches social and economic roles of Sumerian citizens. Challenge each pair to pull its information together and assume the roles of ancient Sumerians with specific social positions (farmer, artisan, trader, priest, slave and so on). Gender and age should be considered as well. Students may present their findings in the form of a detailed daily planner to show their characters' routine activities and the related gods and goddesses to which they may have prayed.

### THOSE INVENTIVE ANCIENTS

Engage students in a discussion about the ways a civilization like that of Mesopotamia may be a site of technological development, in contrast to a smaller, less-settled society. Invite each student to compose a page of a class book describing the history and importance of one invention or innovation developed by Sumerians. Some areas for research include architecture (the ziggurat), farming (the plow and irrigation systems), writing (cuneiform), trade (the wheel and the sail), religious practice, and the development of codes of laws.

## RESOURCES

### BOOKS

*Science in Ancient Mesopotamia (Science of the Past)* by Carol Moss (Franklin Watts, 1998)

*Mesopotamia (Cultures of the Past)* by Pamela F. Service (Marshall Cavendish, 1998)

### WEBSITE

Awesome Library

    (www.awesomelibrary.com/Classroom/Social_Studies/History/Ancient_and_Medieval.html)
    Select "Ancient Mesopotamians" for lesson plans, links to other websites, images, and maps
    related to Mesopotamia.

# SARGON'S RULE AND HAMMURABI'S CODE

## CHARACTERS

**Storyteller   Sargon   King Zagesi**
**Hammurabi   Babylonian Woman   Babylonian Man**

*Scene 1: Sumeria in 2350 BC*

**STORYTELLER:** Almost everyone agrees that Sargon was a harsh ruler. One by one, he conquered the city-states of Mesopotamia—Uruk, Lagash, Ur, Umma. The walls of each city-state came tumbling down as Sargon put its people under his rule. Some say he was abandoned as a baby by the water's edge; then he became a gardener; later, he served the King of Kish—

**SARGON:** *(To Zagesi, as if finishing his story)* . . . until I got sick and tired of being ordered around by the king, and I killed him. Then I took over the entire Kish kingdom. Now I am in charge of many city-states and am more powerful than anyone! . . . But look at it this way, Zagesi, you don't have to worry anymore. No more decisions, no more trouble. The city-state of Umma—your *former* dominion—is in my hands now.

**ZAGESI:** You can write your name and put a star in front of it, Sargon, but that doesn't make you a king. A king has wisdom. A king uses his power well.

**SARGON:** What's wrong, Zagesi? Don't you enjoy wearing a dog collar? You really look quite handsome in it. The people of Umma will understand your new role when they see you wearing your collar and walking with me.

**ZAGESI:** You'll never be able to hold an empire together. You can imprison me and all the other kings, but the people will rise against you. Your enemies from inside and outside will attack you.

**SARGON:** A strong king need not fear. All my enemies may rise against me, but they'll never defeat me. I've conquered Lagash, Uruk, Ur, and now Umma.

**ZAGESI:** You have not conquered them. You'll see.

**SARGON:** I like you, Zagesi, I really do. I want you to wear your dog collar when you join the other ex-kings in prison. Show it off. You're the only one I've given a collar to. It's an honor, really, to be the pet of King Sargon.

**STORYTELLER:** Zagesi was right: Sargon's empire was plagued by rebellion and invasion. Still, Sargon ruled Mesopotamia for 54 years, until his death. His descendants held the empire for another 59 years, until the year 2250 BC.

Scholastic Professional Books, 2000

*Scene 2: Babylonia in 1700 BC*

**STORYTELLER:** The Sumerians were the first people to develop a written language, but the Babylonians took civilization to new heights in arts and science. In Babylonia, along the banks of the Euphrates River, King Hammurabi developed a set of laws for his people. Hammurabi's Code, carved on a huge slab of basalt, contained 282 laws. This code spelled out punishment for crimes committed against the three classes—nobles, commoners, and slaves—and regulated economic dealings including contracts, wages, and debts.

**HAMMURABI:** Who makes the complaint?

**BABYLONIAN WOMAN:** I do, Your Excellency.

**BABYLONIAN MAN:** Her own fault, Excellency. She didn't jump out of the way in time.

**WOMAN:** You may be a nobleman, but you don't own the road. *(To Hammurabi)* He not only broke my arm, but he also scared my donkey and caused it to run away. I still haven't found it.

**MAN:** The donkey was sitting in the middle of the road. What was I supposed to do? Stop and wait for her to drag him to the side? I'm a busy man.

**WOMAN:** I may be a common woman, but I venture that I'm busier than you are. And now I'm a busy woman who can't do her work because of a broken arm!

**HAMMURABI:** One at a time. Let me hear the injured party's story first.

**WOMAN:** Thank you. I'll be brief. My donkey had a stone in his hoof. As the road is a steep cliff on one side and a steep mountain on the other, I sat him near the mountain edge of the road to examine his hoof. The road is straight, Your Excellency. He saw me from a mile away. What does he do? He shouts for me to get out of the way. His arms are flying and his legs are kicking, and his left leg kicks me in the arm as he gallops past. I had to let go of my poor, terrified mule.

**MAN:** She exaggerates. I barely raised my voice. And my horse is very slow.

**HAMMURABI:** But clearly, your leg is very strong. I command you to pay two minas of silver to this woman, one for injuring her arm and one for the loss of her donkey.

**MAN:** Excellency, really!

**HAMMURABI:** Be glad she wasn't of noble birth. Your punishment would have been a broken arm.

**STORYTELLER:** Which would you rather be ruled by, a strong king or a wise one? And is not a wise king a strong king?

Scholastic Professional Books, 2000

# "SARGON'S RULE AND HAMMURABI'S CODE"

## DISCUSSION QUESTIONS

- What personal and leadership qualities helped Sargon unite the city-states into an empire?
- What do you think of the Storyteller's final questions? In your opinion, did Hammurabi lay down his laws wisely? Did this make him a strong leader, and if so, why?

## ACTIVITIES

### MUSEUM OF KINGS

Challenge students to select a Mesopotamian ruler to feature in a visual display accompanied by written information. To add an authentic flavor to the display, students may use slabs of clay and a stylus-like instrument to inscribe the image of the ruler they have selected as well as a motto or other words that describe his reign. The portrait work may be displayed around the room in chronological order to provide a visual history of royalty in Mesopotamia.

### AN EYE FOR AN EYE . . . AND JUSTICE FOR ALL?

Provide students with a sample list of Hammurabi's laws. Spend some time discussing how trials during the time of Hammurabi were conducted, and compare the Babylonian model with that of current American trials. Then challenge groups of students to re-create the trial depicted in the mini-play, as if in a court today. Alternately, students might examine the following scenario: a builder is accused of faulty construction practices which resulted in a structure collapsing and killing someone. During Hammurabi's time, this builder would be forced to give up his life or his son's life, if found guilty. Challenge students to explore what the outcome might be today.

### LEGALLY SPEAKING

Are laws really necessary? Are they always effective? Encourage your students to explore these questions by dividing the class into small groups and presenting them with a simple, familiar activity, like making a peanut butter and jelly sandwich. Then assign each group to do the activity according to a particular method of lawmaking. For example, provide one group with a very clear set of laws that arbitrarily favor certain students (e.g., give more or less responsibility to those with long hair, those wearing blue, and so on). Allow another group to vote on a set of laws before they begin the activity. Challenge a third group to proceed without any guidelines (except normal classroom safety expectations). Direct a fourth group to follow laws set by only one or two group leaders. Laws can govern all parts of the activity, from who performs certain tasks to how materials are to be shared. If time allows, have the groups do the activity again under a different type of "legal system." Close with students' reactions to these different systems.

## RESOURCES

### BOOKS

*Gilgamesh the King* by Ludamila Zeman (Tundra Books, 1998). Adapted from the epic story of a hero-king of Uruk, compiled around 2,000 BC.

*You Be the Jury* series by Marvin Miller (Scholastic, 1987)

### MAGAZINE

"Mesopotamia." *Kids Discover Magazine*, Vol. 9, No. 11 (November 1999)

### WEBSITE

Internet Ancient History Sourcebook (www.fordham.edu/halsall/ancient/asbook.html )
    Select links to text of Hammurabi's Code, Babylonian maps, art, politics, and language.

# PLANNING A PYRAMID

## CHARACTERS

**Narrator    King Zoser    Vizier    Khnum    Imhotep    Builders 1–2**

*Scene 1: In the Egyptian capital city of Memphis, c. 2700 BC*

**NARRATOR:** In ancient Egypt, pharaohs had absolute power. A pharaoh was considered to be a god on earth, who had control over all Egyptians and their land—including the mighty Nile River. On this day, however, the pharaoh Zoser was feeling more like an ordinary man than a god.

**ZOSER:** When will it rain? The Nile must rise soon. My people are starving. Their crops are withering. The sun has baked the land until it is too hard to plow. Khnum, mighty god of the Nile, why do you resist my prayers?

**VIZIER:** Riots have broken out in the city. Neighbors are stealing food from each other. The people are calling for you to do something to end this drought.

**ZOSER:** Do you think I'm deaf and blind? Do you think that I don't see and hear their suffering, hear their babies crying through the night from hunger?

**VIZIER:** But what shall we do?

**ZOSER:** Restore order in the city.

**VIZIER:** But—

**ZOSER:** Go! Do it NOW!

(*The Vizier bows and leaves. Zoser paces.*)

**ZOSER:** The Nile sleeps in two caves deep below the temple just beyond our borders to the south. Khnum, you control the floodgates. Why do you withhold precious water from Egypt? Why do you withhold the rich layers of soil the river leaves behind? Why do you make us suffer through this "low Nile"? (*Yawning*) I'm so tired.

**NARRATOR:** As Zoser slept, he dreamed that the god Khnum spoke to him.

**KHNUM:** I have heard your pleas, Zoser, and those of your people. I *am* the god of the Nile. I know all its secrets. When the river covers the fields, it brings life to them and crops grow. I will release the Nile soon. It will pour over the land. The years of starvation and death will end. Tell your people, Zoser.

Scholastic Professional Books, 2000

**ZOSER:** *(Waking with a start)* Khnum!

**NARRATOR:** According to legend, the "high Nile" returned and the years of hunger ended. Every year the Egyptians remembered the life-giving gifts the river brought them, and they gave thanks to the god Khnum.

*Scene 2: In the desert, outside Memphis, c. 2700 BC*

**NARRATOR:** The ancient Egyptians believed their souls lived on in the afterlife. A proper burial was important to achieve entrance to the afterlife. Zoser thought carefully about how he would be buried. One day the pharaoh called the architect Imhotep to him.

**IMHOTEP:** How may I serve you, Zoser?

**ZOSER:** I have in mind a tomb, something grander than anything that has ever been built before. Not an underground chamber that no one will ever see, but a mighty structure that will last for thousands and thousands of years—a stone structure.

**IMHOTEP:** Such a structure would take thousands of workers and many years.

**ZOSER:** Then you'd better get started right away.

**NARRATOR:** Imhotep designed a structure that the world had never before seen. He turned the traditional burial tomb of the pharaohs inside out and created a step pyramid more than 200 feet tall. Here, he consults with two builders.

**IMHOTEP:** The actual burial chamber will be 80 feet underground. A mile-long wall will surround the tomb.

**BUILDER 1:** A mile long? That's a lot of wall for one tomb . . . but the king will probably like that. And what about these tunnels? What's going on there?

**IMHOTEP:** The burial chamber will have 14 doors, but only one will really open. An underground maze of tunnels will lead to the chamber. The king's body, and his offerings to the gods, must be protected at all costs.

**BUILDER 2:** *(Aside to Builder 1)* Like anybody's going to miss Zoser when he dies.

**BUILDER 1:** Yeah, let him stay in there a while.

**NARRATOR:** Zoser's dream and Imhotep's design began the Pyramid Age, one of Egypt's most creative periods, but not without a heavy price tag in human labor.

# "PLANNING A PYRAMID"

## DISCUSSION QUESTIONS

- The Greek historian Herodotus coined the phrase "gift of the Nile" in reference to Egypt. What geographic factors contributed to the growth and prosperity of early Egypt?
- If you were in King Zoser's position, what kinds of pressures might you feel? What responsibilities would you have to handle? How do these kinds of responsibilities compare to those of a United States president?

## ACTIVITIES

### VOICES BEHIND THE STONES
Invite students to locate graphic, textual, and Internet sources to study both a Mesopotamian ziggurat and an Egyptian pyramid (e.g., the ziggurat at Ur, c. 2100, and the Great Pyramid near Giza, c. 2600 BC). Students may want to build or draw models, with captions, as they learn how these buildings were constructed. Have students write a brief description of their day as a laborer working on one of these structures. Encourage them to include specifics about the material and technology used and their feelings about their jobs and treatment.

### WRAPPING UP HISTORY
Once students have become familiar with the ancient Egyptian mummification process and burial rites, provide them with an opportunity to reenact their own burial. In small groups, instruct students to pretend that one of them is an Egyptian pharaoh or king. The group members should decide what kind of structure this leader will be buried in and design the pyramid on paper, using ancient models, such as Tutankhamen's tomb, as guides. They should list the items to be buried in the tomb and create a model sarcophagus from cardboard. Finally, invite the group to "mummify" the "king" in toilet paper and perform a mock burial, complete with a student-written chant over the mummy.

### JUST YOUR AVERAGE FEAST
In Egyptian documents, experts have located references to more than 50 different types of bread! This suggests quite a bit about the Egyptians' culinary repertoire and the agriculture that supported it. Have students study Egyptian wall paintings describing harvests and feasts and use recipe resources to write a menu for a feast given by a noble. The class or some student volunteers may be able to cook a dish for the class to enjoy.

## RESOURCES

### BOOKS
*Ancient Egypt (See Through History)* by Judith Crosher (Viking, 1993)
*Ancient Egyptian Art (Art in History)* by Susie Hodge (Heinemann Library, 1998)
*Pyramid* by David McCaulay (Houghton Mifflin, 1982)
*Unwrap the Mummy!* by Ian Dicks and David Hancock (Random House, 1995)

### WEBSITE
Ancient Aromas (www.journalnow.com/living/food/worldflavors/egypt142.htm)
Online article by Candide Jones from *Journal Now* (January 14, 1998) includes recipes and information on ancient Egyptian culinary arts.

# HATSHEPSUT AND THUTMOSE III

## CHARACTERS

**Narrator**  **Hatshepsut**  **Thutmose I**  **Thutmose III**  **Vizier**

*The New Kingdom period in Egypt, 1500 BC*

**NARRATOR:** The New Kingdom period in Egypt lasted from about 1600 BC to 1100 BC and is known as the Age of Empire. The Egyptians conquered vast amounts of new territory. Conquered peoples from Nubia, Babylonia, Syria, and Palestine came to the capital, Thebes, to pay tribute in goods to the pharaoh. Hatshepsut (*hat-SHEP-soot*), the daughter of King Thutmose (*thoot-MO-suh*) I, spent a lot of time at the royal court.

**HATSHEPSUT:** If I were pharaoh, I'd send a trade expedition to Punt. Remember the riches the great explorer Hannu returned with—gold, silver, myrrh? Then I'd use those riches to rebuild the old temples that are falling down and build beautiful new ones.

**THUTMOSE I:** That's an ambitious scheme.

**HATSHEPSUT:** A pharaoh should be ambitious.

**THUTMOSE I:** So he should.

**HATSHEPSUT:** A pharaoh must also be a man.

**THUTMOSE I:** So he must . . . but a pharaoh can select the person who shall rule after him. It's not possible for you to become a pharaoh, Hatshepsut, but I've selected you to succeed me, as Queen of Egypt.

**HATSHEPSUT:** I'll do my best for Egypt and my people—but what about the royal nobles? Will they follow me?

**THUTMOSE I:** I've made my wishes known to them. You must do the rest.

**NARRATOR:** Three years later, Thutmose I died, and Queen Hatshepsut began her rule. She took a husband, Thutmose II, but he died after they had been married for seven years. Her stepson Thutmose III was next in line to rule, but Hatshepsut declared herself king and pharaoh. Until Hatshepsut's death, she and Thutmose III co-ruled Egypt.

**THUTMOSE III:** To make a strong and mighty Egypt, we must expand our territory.

Scholastic Professional Books, 2000

**HATSHEPSUT:** We're enjoying peace and prosperity. Tributes pour into Egypt from the lands we've already conquered. Why spoil the balance with war instead of trade?

**THUTMOSE III:** Because I'm a good general. We must take advantage of other countries' weaknesses where we can.

**HATSHEPSUT:** Not while I rule.

**THUTMOSE III:** You say that I rule jointly with you, until I suggest something you oppose.

**HATSHEPSUT:** I've asked you to rule with me as a way of giving you experience. You'll be glad when you and you alone are ruler of Egypt. Learn this and learn it well: Make sure Egypt is strong within before you go outside and create enemies for her.

**THUTMOSE III:** And I say we must attack before we are attacked.

**NARRATOR:** Hatshepsut died in 1482 BC, and Thutmose III became pharaoh.

**THUTMOSE III:** Now, at last, we can expand Egypt's empire! I want all kings and their sons captured, not killed, and sent here to Thebes. We'll keep them close and teach them our ways.

**VIZIER:** Surely that will be seen as a sign of weakness . . . .

**THUTMOSE III:** Show mercy to your enemies, but keep them close.

**VIZIER:** I'm glad Hapshepsut isn't alive to see this.

**THUTMOSE III:** So am I. My stepmother was a wise—and cautious—ruler. Too cautious.

**NARRATOR:** For 30 years Thutmose III successfully ruled and waged war, expanding Egyptian territories and tribute. Many historians honor him with the title Thutmose the Great.

# "HATSHEPSUT AND THUTMOSE III"

## DISCUSSION QUESTIONS

- Hatshepsut and Thutmose III are both considered important New Kingdom pharaohs for their contributions. During which reign would you like to have lived? Why?

- What are qualities that you value in a strong leader? Do these qualities differ for leaders of small groups and leaders of large groups? If so, how and why?

## ACTIVITIES

### AND THE WINNER IS . . .
Pose the following scenario to your class: One Egyptian ruler from the New Kingdom period is going to be inducted into the Ruler Hall of Fame. Half the class will represent Hatshepsut's supporters while the other side will support Thutmose III. Each group will present their ruler to a jury panel of students (perhaps to a group of older students) as the most capable and most deserving of this award. Encourage each side to focus on political, cultural, and economic accomplishments; length of rule; leadership style; and so on. Using a debate forum, let each side present its case to the jury.

### THE QUEEN'S BEAUTIFUL BUILDINGS
Assign students the role of Hatshepsut's architects. Have them research new designs in architecture that occurred in the New Kingdom and specifically under her reign. Encourage students to apply their knowledge of New Kingdom architecture to draw up new temple designs. Simulate a scenario in which each architect/group of architects presents a temple plan to the class as if presenting it to Hatshepsut, her vizier, and her other advisers. Presentations should include reasons for the design of the temple, explaining who will use the building, how it will be used, and what its religious importance will be. The class "council" may want to develop a rubric to evaluate the designs.

### LEADERSHIP REPORT CARD
Ask students to bring in current events articles or locate articles on the Internet and discuss ways in which current world leaders come to and stay in power. Students may select a particular leader to follow in the news over the course of one to two weeks and grade that leader on qualities they think a leader should have, such as strength, wisdom, compassion, and integrity. You may want to design a report-card format by which students grade the leaders according to their chosen criteria and even make comments detailing reasons for the grade.

## RESOURCES

### BOOKS
*Ancient Egyptian Places* by Sarah McNeil and Sarah Howarth (Milbrook, 1997)
*His Majesty, Queen Hatshepsut* by Dorothy S. Carter (Lippincott Williams & Wilkins, 1987)
*The Remarkable Women of Ancient Egypt* by Barbara S. Lesko (BC Scribe, 1996)

### WEBSITE
The Learning Network at *The New York Times* (www.nytimes.com/learning)
    Find student, teacher, and parent resources related to current events.

# MEROË'S WARRIOR QUEEN

### CHARACTERS

**Candace    Dr. Sylvia Earll    Candake Amanirenas**
**Teritekas    Prince Akinidad    Petronius**

**CANDACE:** Are you still trying to figure out what that old tombstone says, Mom? You've been working on it forever.

**DR. SYLVIA EARLL:** It's the tombstone from the grave of Candake Amanirenas (*KAN-duh-kay ah-mah-nuh-RAY-nus*) in Africa. Did you know I named you after her?

**CANDACE:** Mom—duh—my name's Candace, not Canda . . . whatever you said.

**DR. EARLL:** In the kingdom of Kush, a ruler-queen was called a Candake. That's how the name "Candace" came into the English language.

**CANDACE:** Ruler-queen, huh? I like that. So who was this Candake Amani . . . whatever you said.

**DR. EARLL:** She's the woman who defeated the army of the Roman emperor Augustus. She actually led her troops into the Egyptian city of Aswan to fight against the Roman army more than 2,000 years ago—around 23 BC.

**CANDACE:** Wait a minute. She was from Kush, but she fought against the Romans in an Egyptian city? What was going on?

**DR. EARLL:** Well, I'll give you a very fast history lesson. The land of Kush was located south of Egypt on the Nile River. There was a lot of gold in Kush; the Egyptian word for gold was *nub* so the Egyptians referred to Kush as Nubia. Because of Kush's wealth and its trade links, Egypt conquered it about 1550 BC.

**CANDACE:** Mom, this is not fast. There are more than 1,500 years before you get to the important part. What about Candake . . . you-know?

**DR. EARLL:** Okay, in about 724 BC the Kushite king Piye took over Egypt. Then about 50 years later, the Assyrians invaded Egypt. Unfortunately, the Assyrians had iron weapons, and they pushed the Kushites back into Kush. The Kushites moved their capital to Meroë, where there was more rain. It was also on a major trade route. The Kushites learned to smelt iron and make their own weapons. The country flourished under the rule of Candake Amanirenas.

**CANDACE:** Where'd the Romans come from?

Scholastic Professional Books, 2000

**DR. EARLL:** They had conquered Egypt. Augustus decided that Kushites who lived around Aswan should pay taxes. Candake Amanirenas was furious.

(*Candake Amanirenas, Teritekas, Prince Akinidad, and Petronius step out from behind the tombstone.*)

**CANDACE:** Whoa! Hey! Mom!

**CANDAKE AMANIRENAS:** I'll say I was furious. We'd been at peace with Egypt until the Romans arrived. Who did Augustus think he was, taxing my people?

**TERITEKAS:** My wife waited until the Romans were attacked in Arabia. Augustus moved most of his men from Aswan to Arabia.

**PRINCE AKINIDAD:** Then we took Aswan. We said to the Romans, "Forget about us paying you any taxes!" We brought the head from a statue of Augustus here to Meroë and buried it so my mother could walk over him. This kept his power contained.

**CANDAKE AMANIRENAS:** Not quite. The Romans won in Arabia. They returned to attack Aswan and fight on to Meroë.

**TERITEKAS:** We'd learned how to smelt and forge iron into weapons. Meroë was one of the major ironwork centers in the world. But still, the Romans pushed up back to the old capital city of Napata.

**PRINCE AKINIDAD:** My mother was so furious that she took over and marched in front of her soldiers. She led them forward and came up against the Roman general Petronius.

**PETRONIUS:** She was one tough ruler. Augustus said we Romans would stop fighting if she agreed to a settlement. And what a settlement it was.

**CANDAKE AMANIRENAS:** Rome gave us everything we demanded—including the taxes they had taken from my people.

**DR. EARLL:** Candake Amanirenas, since you're here, would you translate your tombstone for me? We haven't been able to decipher the Meroitic (*MEHR-oh-it-ik*) language.

**CANDAKE AMANIRENAS:** Sorry, I can't help you with that. The only thing I can do is tell my story. But I bet my namesake'll be able to help you figure it out one of these days.

# "MEROË'S WARRIOR QUEEN"

## DISCUSSION QUESTIONS

- What does this play tell about the position of women in Kush society?
- How did Kush use the resources available in Meroë to build a major trading and ironworking center?

## RESEARCH ACTIVITIES

### TRADING FROM MEROË

Once students have studied the Meroitic Period (following the Kush move to Meroë), challenge them to apply their understanding of Kushite trade: Have students assume the role of a Kush merchant and create an imaginary log of transactions and business plans over two or more days. The log should reflect knowledge of objects and resources to be traded, peoples with whom the Kush would trade, regions from which goods could be acquired, and types of transportation needed to move the goods. When sharing their logs, students should consider how a new location and new technology, such as the production of iron tools, affected Kushite trade.

### TRADE WEB

In addition or as an alternative to the above project, ask students to create a map that features similar information generated about the Kush trade. The map should show areas rich in resources and/or goods to be traded and trade routes connecting Meroë with those areas and other centers of trade.

### LETTERS FROM THE SHOP

Provide students with resources on iron making and Assyrian weaponry. Invite students to write a letter from an apprentice in an iron workshop in Meroë to a relative back in northern Nubia. Students should be able to describe the iron smelting process, basic properties of iron, ironworking techniques, and the types of tools and weapons that might have been produced.

## RESOURCES

### BOOKS

*The Story of Iron (First Book)* by Karen Fitzgerald (Franklin Watts, 1997)
*Egypt, Kush, Askum; Northeast Africa* by Kenny Mann (Silver Burdette, 1996)
*Nubian Kingdoms (African Civilizations)* by Edna Russman (Franklin Watts, 1999)

# INTO ISRAEL

## CHARACTERS

Narrator    Ramses II    Midwife    Pharaoh's Daughter
Moses    Overseer    Hebrew Men 1–2    Jethro    Hebrew Women 1–2

**NARRATOR:** What we know about the ancient Hebrews comes largely from religious texts, and some of this history is hard to confirm. We do know for a fact that Hebrews who lived in Egypt's New Kingdom in the 13th century BC were in trouble. The pharaoh Ramses II was worried that they would join his enemies and fight him. The following scene retells a biblical story of the Exodus.

**RAMSES II:** Now, listen to me and hear me well. I don't want any Hebrew baby boys to live. Make sure they don't. Tell all the other midwives.

**MIDWIFE:** But, sire—

**RAMSES II:** They're a danger. They worship only one god, not many gods, as we do. They live here in Egypt, yet they don't practice Egyptian ways. I'll see that they do.

**NARRATOR:** A Hebrew woman had a baby boy. To protect her child, she hid him in a basket of bulrushes in a river. Coincidentally, the pharaoh's daughter came to the river that day to bathe.

**PHARAOH'S DAUGHTER:** What's this? A baby! Who left you here, little one? You can't stay here, you'll have to come home with me.

**NARRATOR:** The baby boy, Moses, grew up in the pharaoh's household as if he were the real son of the pharaoh's daughter. Nobody in the royal court knew he was Hebrew by birth. All was well until one day Moses saw an Egyptian overseer beating a Hebrew man.

**MOSES:** Hey—cut it out! You'll kill him if you beat him like that!

**OVERSEER:** I'll kill you if you don't stay out of this!

(*Moses strikes the overseer, who falls down dead.*)

**HEBREW MAN 1:** You killed him! You'd better get out of here—quick!

**NARRATOR:** Moses ran away to a place called Midian in Arabia, where he met Jethro and married Jethro's daughter, Zipporeh. In Midian, Moses learned about the Hebrew God.

Scholastic Professional Books, 2000

**MOSES:** Jethro! There was a fire! A bush was burning! The fire was hot, but it didn't burn the bush! It was God! God spoke to me!

**JETHRO:** Slow down, slow down, Moses. Catch your breath.

**MOSES:** "Your people need you, Moses," he said. "You must free the Hebrews from Egyptian slavery and deliver them to a land of milk and honey, where the Canaanites and other peoples live." "Why me?" I asked. "I'm just a man."

**JETHRO:** You must return to Egypt. You must do what God asks you to do.

**NARRATOR:** Moses returned to Egypt. He met with Ramses II and demanded that all Hebrew people be released from slavery. A series of plagues hit Egypt, which helped convince Ramses to let the Hebrews go.

**HEBREW WOMAN 1:** Where are we going, Moses? How long will it take?

**HEBREW MAN 2:** What's the land like there? Is there plenty of water?

**MOSES:** We must cross the desert. It will be a long, hot journey. Then we must cross the sea.

**HEBREW WOMAN 2:** The sea! How? How are we to do that?

**MOSES:** God will provide the way.

**NARRATOR:** Moses and his people wandered for 40 years in the desert. Life was hard, and the people turned away from Moses and God. On a mountaintop Moses pleaded with God not to abandon the Hebrew people. Moses received a decree from God to share the Ten Commandments with his people.

**MOSES:** You must renew your faith in God, my people. Read these commandments, which He carved into stone. This is what God expects of us.

**HEBREW MAN 1:** (*Reading from a stone tablet*) Thou shalt not kill . . . Thou shalt not steal . . . I promise to keep these commandments.

**HEBREW WOMAN 1:** These are righteous commandments. I too promise to follow them!

**NARRATOR:** Moses finally led the Hebrew people to the Jordan River. He climbed to the top of Mount Pisgah and saw the promised land across the river. But Moses died on the mountain and his people never saw him again. A man named Joshua led the Hebrew people across the river, into Israel.

# "INTO ISRAEL"

## DISCUSSION QUESTIONS

• Think about ethical teachings you've heard of or learned. Are any of these teachings related to the Ten Commandments? Which ones are and how?

• How would you compare the Hebrews' monotheistic beliefs to those of the Egyptians and other polytheistic groups in the Middle East?

## ACTIVITIES

### MOSAIC OF THE HEBREWS
Use a mosaic motif as a way to represent Jewish history in a unified design. On a large piece of butcher paper, have students sketch out events, people, and symbols from Jewish history, beginning with the time of the Hebrews. You may want to organize students in groups that cover different periods in history. Allow each group a segment of the mosaic to complete. When groups have sketched their designs, invite them to paste in bits of colored craft paper to complete the image, in true mosaic fashion. Allow groups time to present their sections of the mosaic.

### PRESS CONFERENCE!
Bring the historic events of Israel's beginnings alive by helping the students to imagine that Moses, Ramses II, and Jethro have been transported to our modern age where the media cover every significant event and report it. Choose three different students to play these historic figures and help them research their backgrounds while the rest of the class prepares to be members of the media at a press conference. They should construct questions for these three students, take notes during the press conference, and then either write articles based on what they learned or prepare mock television broadcasts.

### WHOSE LAND IS IT?
Arguments over rights to land that is considered sacred by different religious groups in the Middle East has caused conflicts between Israelis and their Middle Eastern neighbors for years. Challenge students to research the continuing conflict over rights to land in the Middle East. Ask students which groups believe they have rights to land and why. As the class follows current events on peace talks, discuss ways groups can negotiate when religion plays such a large role in claims to territory.

## RESOURCES

### BOOKS
*Clouds of Glory: Jewish Legends and Stories About Bible Times* by Miriam Chalkin (Clarion, 1996)

*Remarkable Jewish Women: Rebels, Rabbis, and Other Women From Biblical Times to the Present* by Emily Taitz with Sandra Henry (Jewish Publication Society, 1996)

*The Young Reader's Encyclopedia of Jewish History* edited by Ilana Shamir (Viking, 1987)

### WEBSITE
The Law Museum Archives (www.wwlia.org/tencomm.htm)
    Text of the Ten Commandments, available through the World Wide Legal Information Association.

# THE PERSIAN EMPIRE

## CHARACTERS

**Cyrus    Darius I    Satraps 1–3    Generals 1–4**

**CYRUS:** Conquering other people and their land is one thing; trying to govern them is another. I should know. I'm Cyrus the Great. I ruled the Persian Empire—and expanded its reach—from 557 BC to my death in battle in 530 BC. That's right—it's the year 518 BC and I've been dead for 12 years. But I like to look in on my successor, Darius I, every once in a while to see how he's doing.

**GENERAL 1:** The rebellions in the Empire are dying down, but some people still think that you can be overthrown and assassinated, just as you did to Gaumata.

**DARIUS I:** Gaumata had no right to seize power when Cyrus' son died. I had to act quickly to keep our Empire strong and intact, and now the Persian Empire extends from the Aegean Sea all the way to the Indus River.

**SATRAP 1:** A wise move, Excellency, if I may say, minting gold coins when we need money AND fixing values for our money. Now everybody knows just how much each coin is worth. VERY smart, Excellency. The Lydians may have been the first to use coins, but you, Excellency, have made the system PERFECT.

**SATRAP 2:** Are you finished? Because I have some serious business to discuss. The people in my province—

**SATRAP 1:** And wasn't that a BRILLIANT move? Dividing the empire into 20 satrapies, each one run by an honest man, such as myself—

**SATRAP 2:** The people in my province say the roads are in need of repair. If the roads are in bad shape, then it's harder for the messengers to get through with the mail.

**SATRAP 1:** Well, what do you expect? The Assyrians built those roads. If Excellency had built those roads, then they would be in PERFECT shape.

**SATRAP 2:** The people in my province feel that since they pay taxes, they should have better roads.

**DARIUS I:** They're right. Get me a list of the roads and what repairs are necessary. Tell your people that I plan on building even more roads.

Scholastic Professional Books, 2000

**SATRAP 3:** What about the canal, Your Excellency? Is it true you're going to build a canal connecting the Nile and the Red Sea?

**DARIUS I:** The canal will build our trade immensely.

**SATRAP 1:** What a CLEVER idea! We have all those ships from conquering the Phoenicians AND the Greeks AND the Egyptians—

**CYRUS:** Let me give you a little background while this satrap yaps on. Between us, Darius and I conquered a large number of territories. I took Assyria, Lydia, Babylonia, and Palestine. I let the Jews who had been exiled to Babylonia return to Jerusalem. Darius is expanding the Empire, moving west to Macedonia and east to the Punjab and Indus Valley.

**SATRAP 1:** It is an HONOR to report to Excellency's officials on my little province when they come to visit. I love reporting to the "Eyes and Ears of the King."

**GENERAL 2:** I wonder, sometimes, if it's such a good idea to choose satraps who live in the provinces they're to govern. Wouldn't it be better to select someone from here and send them to the provinces?

**DARIUS I:** The people must trust their satraps. Just as I must trust my satraps to give me accurate information, and not useless compliments.

**SATRAP 1:** That is SO wise, Excellency. I—

**DARIUS I:** Tell me something useful, Satrap.

**SATRAP 1:** There is NO rebellion in my province. We are sending 200 soldiers to serve Your Excellency. We have paid our yearly tribute early, AND we have enough money left over to build six more post houses along the highway for travelers.

**GENERAL 3:** Things in your province may be fine, but I'm worried about the Greeks.

**GENERAL 4:** You always worry about the Greeks.

**CYRUS:** The general is wise to worry about the Greeks. Greece will indeed rise against Persian rule. It will mean the end of the great Persian Empire . . .

**DARIUS I:** We have a large empire, with many different peoples and customs and cultures. Cyrus the Great understood that you had to allow certain freedoms to the people you conquer while maintaining a strong government with strong laws. I understand that, too. I want my generals and satraps to worry aloud to me. I need my "eyes and ears" to be everywhere in my Empire.

**CYRUS:** Well, Satrap 1 is right. Darius is a wise man. He continues my work, and will until his death in 486 BC.

# "THE PERSIAN EMPIRE"

## DISCUSSION QUESTIONS

• What were some new and important ways Persian kings united their huge empire? Why do you think these strategies worked so well, particularly in comparison to the harsh techniques that characterized Assyrian rule?

• What are some problems in governing ethnically diverse populations? What kinds of advantages as well as problems exist today in diverse countries like the United States?

## ACTIVITIES

### EMPIRE EXPANSION

How do cartographers represent different political territories in the same area on a single map? Invite students to illustrate maps to show the sizes of the Assyrian and Persian Empires. Students should make decisions about the use of color and line to describe the territory possessed by each empire at its height. Other map information might include the territory of conquered groups and important leaders. A few students might focus on the gradual growth of the Persian state from the rule of Cyrus the Great through the wars with Greece, showing the shifts of both states' boundaries. Finished maps make excellent visual resources to hang in the room or keep with their history materials as study sheets.

### SO MANY DIFFERENT PEOPLE!

Studying the variety of groups contributing to the culture of the Middle East during the early Iron Age can be overwhelming. Invite students to form interest-based groups that focus on one of the peoples represented in the play (Hittites, Lydians, Assyrians, Phoenicians, Hebrews, and so on). Assign each group a ten-minute presentation on the history, regions, and unique features of it's chosen people. Presentations should include at least one visual aid.

### TOUGH AS . . . IRON!

The innovations that the Hittites made in ironworking helped to initiate an era known as the Iron Age, which continues today. Encourage students to investigate the differences in quality and endurance between stone tools, later bronze tools, and the more advanced iron tools. If possible, have pieces of stone, bronze, and iron available for students to compare and talk about. Students will benefit from preparing questions about ancient and modern building materials and practices for an engineer, who could be invited to speak, or receive and respond to questions online or by mail.

## RESOURCES

### BOOKS

*The Assyrian Empire* edited by Don Nardo (Lucent Books, 1998)
*The Persian Empire* edited by Don Nardo (Lucent Books, 1998)
*Weapons and Warfare: From the Stone Age to the Space Age* by Milton Meltzer (HarperCollins Juvenile, 1996)

### WEBSITE

Cyrus the Great by Nadir Seif (www.oznet.net.net/cyrus/)
Provides background information, translated text of Cyrus the Great's "Charter of the Rights of Nations," a bas relief image of Cyrus the Great, and more.

# TO THE EAST:
# INDIA AND CHINA

## SETTING THE STAGE: MINI-PLAYS 11, 12, 13, 14, 15, AND 16

Section III focuses on cultural developments from early civilizations through the classical era in present-day India and China. The first three plays introduce the beginning of Indian society with the encounter of two cultures, the Aryans and Indus River Valley peoples, and the emergence of two important religions, Hinduism and Buddhism. The last three plays highlight competing schools of thought in late Zhou China, the policies and achievements of the Q'in Dynasty, and the social order of the Han Dynasty.

## BACKGROUND

In search of land and animals for herding, bands of nomads from present-day Pakistan migrated to the Indus River Valley region in the middle of the second millennium BC. These warlike Aryans brought experience in raising livestock and maintained a polytheistic religious tradition passed on through age-old hymns and chants. **"Aryans in the Indus River Valley"** highlights the clash of this invading culture with that of the peaceful, agrarian Indus River Valley peoples, who lived in well-planned, urban centers. The reason for the decline of the Indus River Valley civilization around the time of the Aryan migrations is debated among historians—did the Aryans simply overrun them or did droughts or other natural disasters cause the decline?

Over the next several hundred years, the Aryans began to settle in the region and a more fixed social order, a caste system that linked social status, privilege, and duty, began to emerge. The Aryan's Vedic religion merged with local traditions to produce Hinduism, a religion now practiced by one out of six people in the world. **"Class and Duty in the Hindu Religion"** represents a popular scene from the *Bhagava-Gita*, a nonscriptural Hindu text recorded between 500 and 200 BC. According to the story, the warrior prince Arjuna reflects on his dharma, or duty to his caste, and makes a choice between his responsibility as a warrior and saving the lives of his family members.

A later religious movement originated in 6th century BC India with a very different prince. **"Buddhism Begins"** dramatizes the life of Siddhartha Gautama, who left his family and worldly possessions to gain enlightenment. He is said to have achieved enlightenment when he adopted a moderate "middle path." As the Buddha, or "Enlightened One," he advocated against the caste system, spoke in the language of the common people, and broke with many other Hindu customs he thought unjust. One of his most important followers was Emperor Ashoka, who in the 3rd century adopted Buddhism as the official religion of the Indian Empire.

Around 2000 BC, early, agriculturally based Chinese society began to organize under dynastic rule along the banks of the Yellow River. Each dynasty, or family of successive rulers, came to power by overthrowing the less powerful incumbents and claiming to have been divinely appointed according to the Mandate of Heaven. By the 3rd century BC, the cultural climate supported the development of competing schools of religion and philosophy. **"Schools of Thought in China"** spotlights three major schools of thought, Confucianism, Taoism, and Legalism, whose spiritual and practical messages challenged the existing social order and the governmental bureaucracy which had become inefficient and nepotistic in the late Zhou period.

**"The Q'in Dynasty,"** set in the late 3rd century BC, features the infamous emperor Q'in Shi Huangdi, who took Legalist policies to an extreme. With the help of his trusted adviser, Li Si, he built an image around his title, First Emperor, that signified unprecedented power and status. Sweeping changes in the language and political infrastructure centralized imperial power and severely limited individual freedom. Q'in Shi Huangdi's best-known achievements include the Great Wall and a complete, human-scale terra-cotta replica of his army. However, his achievements came at a political price.

Soldier and peasant rebellions following Q'in Shi Huangdi's death put a quick end to the Q'in Dynasty in 202 BC. The new Han Dynasty (202 BC–220 AD) ushered in a period of expanded trade, fewer governmental extremes, and renewed Confucian ideals, including the first Civil Service Exam given to scholar-officials. Despite the increased power of the individual, not all people enjoyed high living standards. Large gaps between the urban elite and the rural poor existed. The final play in this section, **"A Tale of Two Chinas,"** describes the stark differences between these two classes.

# ARYANS IN THE INDUS RIVER VALLEY

## CHARACTERS

**Chuck Hudson**     **Ruth Varadhan**     **Spike Lewis**
**Indus River Valley (IRV) People 1–2**     **Aryans 1–2**

**CHUCK HUDSON:** Welcome to America's number one history game show, "What Really Happened Anyway?" Tonight our subject is the downfall of the Indus River Valley culture in ancient India. Did the Aryans storm in and take over, or was it nature—droughts, floods—that brought this once-mighty civilization to an end?

**IRV 1:** It was the Aryans' fault, no question about it.

**CHUCK:** Ohh-kay, we're off to an early start. Let me just finish the introduction, pal, and then you can lay it all out for us. On one side (thanks to the wonders of time travel and virtual reality), we have Dr. Spike Lewis and his team—two Indus River Valley people; on the other side, Dr. Ruth Varadhan and her team—two Aryans. Okay, the Aryan team won the toss. Dr. Varadhan?

**RUTH VARADHAN:** The Aryans had nothing to do with it. The Indus River kept flooding or perhaps changed its course. There may have been severe drought.

**SPIKE LEWIS:** Wrong. The Aryans came charging in and took over everything.

**ARYAN 1:** Those Irvs were going down the tubes before we even rode over the Hindu Kush mountains and south into the Indus River Valley.

**CHUCK:** Hold on—Irvs?

**ARYAN 2:** Irvs—Indus River Valley people.

**IRV 2**: Do you hear that? Do you? The Aryans always show us disrespect.

**ARYAN 1:** Aryans are herders. What would we want with your cities?

**CHUCK:** Ohh-kay. Team captains, try to keep your players in line. Dr. Lewis, go ahead and state your case.

**SPIKE:** The Indus River people flourished between 2500 BC and 1600 BC. In 1920 two of their great cities, Harappa and Mohenjodaro (*moh-hen-jo-DAH-roh*), were discovered by archaeologists. They were ports and centers of trade with the Middle East. They had granaries filled with wheat grown on the banks of the Indus River. Each city had a geometric grid of streets. Houses had inner courtyards—

Scholastic Professional Books, 2000

**IRV 1:** *And* indoor plumbing. What do herders know about indoor plumbing?

**RUTH:** But how do you explain what happened to each city? The people of Harappa seem to have disappeared almost overnight, while Mohenjodaro deteriorated over a period of time.

**ARYAN 2:** Right. The Irvs brought about their own downfall. For one thing, they let their herds overgraze the land. That's bad for crops. No crops, nothing to eat, or to trade.

**ARYAN 1:** We Aryans built our own villages, small at first. They grew into cities. We began our own trade.

**SPIKE:** At least the Indus River Valley people *had* cities to leave behind. Archaeologists like me know a lot more about their history than we do about the Aryans. Show me an Aryan city or a piece of Aryan art that anybody's ever found.

**RUTH:** Read the *Rig-Veda*. It tells all about the Aryans.

**SPIKE:** I agree that it's a beautiful work of literature, but what does it tell us about the everyday life of the Aryans? Nothing. It's a series of 1,028 hymns that describes sacrifices to the gods and other religious rites.

**IRV 2:** Don't forget about the caste system. Tell them about the caste system.

**SPIKE:** The Aryan society was divided into three classes, or castes: nobles, priests, and ordinary people. Eventually, there was a fourth class, the warriors.

**ARYAN 1:** But people from different castes could mingle together. You could move to a different caste. It's wasn't like the caste system India has today.

**IRV 1:** The Aryans were always fighting each other, too. They set up their own kingdoms and tried to take over each other's territory.

**RUTH:** If the Aryans were always fighting each other, then when would they have had time to band together to drive out the Indus River Valley people?

**SPIKE:** They drove out the Indus River Valley people and *then* started to fight over the land—

**CHUCK:** Oops! Sorry, we're out of time, folks! You be the judge—what really happened to the Indus River Valley civilization?

# "ARYANS IN THE INDUS RIVER VALLEY"

## DISCUSSION QUESTIONS

• What were the major differences between the Aryans and Indus River Valley cultures?
• Name several factors that make it difficult to figure out what might have happened to the Indus River Valley people?

## ACTIVITIES

### FROM THE EVIDENCE PROVIDED, WE CAN ASSUME . . .

Present students with archaeological evidence from major Indus River Valley societies like Harappa and Mohenjodaro, and invite students to suggest what this evidence can tell us about the quality of life for this civilization. Take the class on a virtual tour of an excavated site (see resources below) or simply provide a list of artifacts on chart paper at the front of the room. The artifact list might include the following: a piece of woven cloth, pieces of turquoise jewelry, pottery fragments, ivory, wide streets, canals leading from water sources to fields, buildings with drainage pipes leading to drainage ditches in the streets. In a whole class discussion or in groups, students can draw conclusions about the quality of life an urban dweller in the Indus River Valley might have enjoyed.

### WHAT A MOVE!

Help your students understand the difficulties of moving to a new environment, such as the Aryans faced when they migrated to the Indus River Valley. Conduct your lesson in a unusual location that does not accommodate the class easily or have all the conveniences of your classroom, like student desks or a chalkboard. Elicit student response to the following questions: *What difficulties did you face when you moved to this new classroom space? What parts of the old classroom environment have you become used to? How would you have to adjust if we held class regularly in this space?* Another variation on this activity involves switching classes with another teacher without warning your students. These situations will facilitate student participation in discussions related to the difficulties of migration.

### MAPPING A MIGRATION

Challenge students to use a variety of nonfiction sources to map out a route that Aryans might have followed as they moved into the Indus River Valley region. The maps should show a departure point in the area of Pakistan to an Indus River Valley destination via the present-day Kush mountain range. In addition to showing possible routes the Aryans may have taken, students can estimate the length of the journey on horseback and describe what the Aryans might have brought with them (food sources, weaponry, clothing, and so on).

## RESOURCES

### BOOK
*Civilizations of the Indus Valley and Beyond* by Mortimer Wheeler (McGraw-Hill, 1972)

### WEBSITES
The Ancient Indus Valley (www.harappa.com/welcome.html)
   Take a slide tour of Harappa and view images from Mohenjodaro.
Indus Valley Civilizaton–A Social Studies/Language Arts Lesson
   (http://members.aol.com/WERedu/PlanIndia.html)
   Access story and lesson plans about daily life and culture in Harappa.

# CLASS AND DUTY IN THE HINDU RELIGION

## CHARACTERS

**Kaurava Cousins 1-3      Yudhisthir      Arjuna      Krishna**

*Scene 1: A game between Yudhisthir and his Kaurava cousins*

**COUSIN 1:** *(Aside to Cousins 2 and 3)* Let's see if we can outsmart our foolish cousin Yudhisthir. What shall we have him wager—and lose—on this game?

**COUSIN 2:** All his weapons . . . . No, let's have him bet the whole kingdom.

**COUSIN 3:** Perfect! I'm in.

**COUSIN 1:** We'll distract him with flattery. Follow my lead. *(To Yudisthir)* You're such a skillful player, Yudhisthir.

**COUSIN 2:** You must be bored playing with your cousins, and winning all the time.

**COUSIN 3:** What can we do to make the game more fun for you, Yudhisthir? I know! We could try throwing the dice with our feet instead of our hands!

**YUDHISTHIR:** Calm down, cousin. Why don't we place wagers on the game?

**COUSIN 1:** I don't know. You have so much, Yudhisthir, a whole kingdom. What do we poor Kauravas have that we can bet?

**COUSIN 2:** You know that Yudhisthir is a fair man, especially to his family. He wouldn't take advantage of us.

**COUSIN 3:** It's just a game, after all. It's not like we would really take all of Yudhisthir's kingdom if he bet it.

**YUDHISTHIR:** Well then, I will wager all the villages of my kingdom.

**COUSIN 1:** Just to make it more interesting—if we win, then you have to go into exile, leave, for 14 years. We'll give everything back to you after that.

**YUDHISTHIR:** *(Laughing)* I thought my Kaurava cousins liked me! Wouldn't you miss me if I went away?

**COUSIN 2:** Of course we would! We only make such an outrageous bet because you're such an excellent player. We know we have no chance of winning.

Scholastic Professional Books, 2000

*(Yudhisthir throws the dice.)*

**COUSIN 3:** Oh, too bad, Yudhisthir. You lose. We'll take good care of your kingdom while you're gone. Fourteen years isn't such a long time!

**YUDHISTHIR:** Hey, wait a minute!

*(The three cousins drag Yudhisthir away.)*

*Scene 2: Fourteen years later, on a battlefield*

**ARJUNA:** First, my Kaurava cousins trick my brother out of his kingdom, and then they refuse to give it back to us Pandavas as they promised. I'm ready for battle, Lord Krishna, my divine charioteer, but first I want to look at my enemies who are so eager to fight.

**KRISHNA:** There they are, Arjuna. Look long and hard.

*(Arjuna stares into the distance and then drops his bow and arrows.)*

**ARJUNA:** I . . . I see fathers and grandfathers, teachers, uncles, brothers, sons, grand-sons, friends. I see my own family. Despite their greed, they are not my enemies. I can't fight them. If we must fight, then let them kill me.

**KRISHNA:** You must fulfill your duty, Arjuna. Your body may die, or theirs, but your souls will continue along the path. You'll take on a new body just as you put on a new set of clothes.

**ARJUNA:** I can't do it.

**KRISHNA:** Arjuna, you were born into the warrior caste. Your duty is to be a warrior. You must fight. Every Hindu must carry out his or her duty, even if it means turning against the ones you love.

**ARJUNA:** How can it be my duty to kill my own family? How can we kill each other over a kingdom?

**KRISHNA:** Pick up your bow and arrows, Arjuna. Great warriors will think you're a coward. It will be a sin if you don't fight. You're a Hindu. You know this: When you're born, you know you'll die. When you're dying, you know you'll be reborn.

*(Arjuna picks up his bow and arrows.)*

**ARJUNA:** You're right, Wise Krishna. I must do my duty as a warrior. I must fight, without any thought of victory or defeat. I will obey your command.

*(Arjuna aims his weapon.)*

# "CLASS AND DUTY IN THE HINDU RELIGION"

## DISCUSSION QUESTIONS

• Have you ever had a responsibility that directed you to act in an unpopular way?
• Describe some important aspects of Hinduism. How is Hinduism like and unlike other religions you've studied?

## ACTIVITIES

### PASS IT ON!

In the oral tradition of early Hinduism, invite students to memorize a favorite Hindu tale (they may want to select the scene of this play found in the *Bhagavad-Gita*) to perform in a five-minute oral presentation. They can present to the whole class, trade stories in small peer groups, or share them with a younger age group. Discussion following each presentation should highlight the ethical advice each story offers. As an extension, such a discussion could be connected with texts from other religions that students have previously studied, such as Buddhist and Jewish legends and stories (see pages 35 and 49).

### AWARD THE WARRIOR?

Present the following scenario to students: Arjuna has been nominated to receive the Most Exemplary Warrior Award, a great honor. Have them decide whether Arjuna is worthy of this honor: Has he stayed true to his duty as a warrior, or has fighting against his family disqualified him? Have small groups of students write short speeches to persuade a panel of peer judges to give or deny this award to Arjuna. Encourage students to consider concepts of heroism, bravery, loyalty, duty, and honor in their speeches.

### THE LAWS OF MANU

The Laws of Manu, developed between 1280 and 880 BC, is a compilation of Hindu legal rules that detail India's caste system. Share excerpts with students and have them discuss the expectations and codes of behavior (dharma) for each caste. Invite students to consider why punishments for people in higher castes are more severe than for those in lower castes. Have students suggest reasons why the religiously based social order has been maintained for thousands of years. For an extension, students might research how practices associated with the caste system in India have changed, especially over the last century with the influence of Gandhi and British government.

## RESOURCES

### BOOKS

*The Adventures of Young Krishna: The Blue God of India* by Diksha Dalal-Clayton (Oxford University Press Children's Books, 1997)

*Hindu (Beliefs & Cultures* series*)* by Anita Ganeri (Children's Press, 1997)

*The Laws of Manu (Penguin Classic)* translated by Wendy Doniger (Penguin, 1992)

### WEBSITES

Caste in Stone?: Examining the Caste System and Its Effects on Indian Society
(www.nytimes.com/learning/teachers/lessons/globalhistory.html)
Full lesson plan with related May 1999 *New York Times* news articles.

The Caste System (www.indiagov.org/Gandhi1/castesystem.htm)
Mahatma Gandhi's 1920 defense and critique of the caste system. The last paragraph deals with his position on "untouchables."

# BUDDHISM BEGINS

## CHARACTERS

| | Narrator | King | Priests 1–3 |
| --- | --- | --- | --- |
| Siddhartha Gautama | Elderly Person | Mourners 1–2 | Followers 1–3 |

**NARRATOR:** Siddhartha Gautama was born in about 560 BC in a kingdom in northern India. His father, the king, consulted priests about his son's future.

**KING:** What's in store for my son? I want him to inherit and rule my kingdom.

**PRIEST 1:** Oh, yes, he will become a great ruler, Sire.

**PRIEST 2:** He will be a great man. People will speak of him long after his death.

**PRIEST 3:** He will lead and guide people, it's true, but not as a king. Seeing the suffering of others, Siddhartha will give up all his worldly possessions and lead a spiritual life. This is how he will guide people.

**KING:** My son will *not* turn his back on everything I've given him. He'll follow in my footsteps—I'll make sure of that! My son will never see sickness or death or poverty. *Never.* From this moment on, only happy and healthy people will be allowed to travel on royal roads.

**PRIEST 3:** You cannot change your son's destiny.

**KING:** Oh, really? Just watch me.

**NARRATOR:** For 29 years Siddhartha was shielded from suffering. But one day, he ventured out beyond his palace. What he saw changed his life forever.

**ELDERLY PERSON:** What are you staring at, young prince? Haven't you ever seen an elderly person before?

**SIDDHARTHA:** I've seen my father grow old, but he—

**ELDERLY PERSON:** He's a king. Kings don't grow old the same way that poor people do.

*(The two mourners enter.)*

**SIDDHARTHA:** What are those people doing?

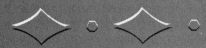

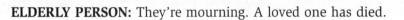

**ELDERLY PERSON:** They're mourning. A loved one has died.

**SIDDHARTHA:** Mourning?

**MOURNER 1:** My beloved uncle has passed away.

**SIDDHARTHA:** I'm sorry.

**MOURNER 2:** He was a good man. He was poor, but he helped others.

*(Siddhartha watches as the mourners leave.)*

**SIDDHARTHA:** I don't know anything about the world.

**NARRATOR:** Siddhartha left the comfort of his palace and went into the world to understand life. He became an ascetic, someone who gives up material things and practices self-denial. Then Siddhartha began to see that moderation was a better way than self-denial. Called the Buddha (the Enlightened One) by his followers, he traveled across India and taught moderation, meditation, and nonviolence.

**FOLLOWER 1:** The Buddha preaches against the caste system. I like that. That makes everyone equal.

**FOLLOWER 2:** I can understand what he says. He speaks in our language instead of Sanskrit. I can't understand Sanskrit. Only the upper castes speak Sanskrit.

**FOLLOWER 3:** And he doesn't expect us to sacrifice animals. That's a nice change—

**FOLLOWER 1:** Shhh! Here he comes!

**SIDDHARTHA:** Best among paths is the eight-fold path: right view, right intentions, right speech, right action, right livelihood, right effort, right mindfulness, right concentration. This path will lead to wisdom, ethics, and awareness.

**FOLLOWER 1:** You're a great man, Buddha.

**SIDDHARTHA:** A Buddha can only point the way. I am only a teacher. Become a lamp unto yourself. The seeker who sets upon the way shines bright over the world.

**FOLLOWER 2:** I'll spread the word.

**FOLLOWER 3:** So will I.

**NARRATOR:** Buddha's followers did spread the word, and his teachings became known as Buddhism. Today Buddhism is the fourth largest religion in the world.

# "BUDDHISM BEGINS"

## DISCUSSION QUESTIONS

• Name three reasons Buddhism appealed to people, particularly in the lower castes.
• What are some ways Buddhism is different from Hinduism?

## ACTIVITIES

### PICTURING BUDDHISM

Have students research the Four Truths and the Noble Eight-fold Path of Buddhism. Challenge students to illustrate a cartoon or poster focusing on these principles. Captions should accompany illustrations. Have students consider different formats for the visual presentation. For example, instead of a typical rectangular format, consider a circular wheel divided into four sections that corresponds to the Four Truths or a cut-out Boddhi tree with eight branches to represent the Eight-fold Path.

### PATHS OF BUDDHISM AND HINDUISM

From India, both Buddhism and Hinduism spread to other lands. Invite students to study how and where each religion spread and draw arrows on maps of Asia to show these routes. Students can use different colors to distinguish the two paths. Extend the activity by having students locate present-day countries where Buddhism and Hinduism are practiced and find out whether both religions are still practiced most frequently in India.

### ASHOKA'S CHOICE: PEACE AND A NEW RELIGION

In the 3rd century BC, Emperor Ashoka abandoned his brutal imperialism, converted to Buddhism, and declared Buddhism the official religion of the Empire. After students have conducted some research on the Maurya period, introduce them to selections from the rock edicts of Ashoka and encourage them to analyze the edicts for Ashoka's outlook and his expectations for Indian society and religion. Discuss how these new laws departed from Hindu law (students who have studied the Laws of Manu may want to compare selections from the two documents).

## RESOURCES

### BOOKS

*Buddha Stories* by Demi (Henry Holt, 1997)
*Buddhist (Cultures and Beliefs)* by Anita Ganeri (Children's Press, 1997)
*The Edicts of Ashoka: An English Rendering* translated by Ven S. Dhammika (Buddhist Publication Society, 1993)

### WEBSITE

PBS Frontline (www.pbs.org/wgbh/pages/frontline/shows/tibet/understand/)
Offers information on Buddhism, the history of Buddhism in Tibet, the Dalai Lama, and current issues.

# SCHOOLS OF THOUGHT IN CHINA

## CHARACTERS

**Prince    Confucian Scholar    Taoist Scholar    Legalist Scholar**

**PRINCE:** Nobody tells me what to do or how to think. *I* am the one who tells people what to do, whether they're Chinese peasants who work for me or barbarians whose land I've taken.

**CONFUCIAN SCHOLAR:** Nobody tells you what to do? Not even the Emperor of the Zhou Dynasty who gave you such power? What would your ancestors say about your behavior?

**PRINCE:** Who cares what they would say?

**CONFUCIAN SCHOLAR:** I care. Confucius (*kuhn-FYOO-shuhs*) would care. He would say that you're not striving for a just and harmonious society. Those who rule must be smart. They must work hard.

**PRINCE:** I am, and I do, so what are you complaining about?

**LEGALIST SCHOLAR:** Intelligence has nothing to do with being a good ruler, my foolish friends. A ruler must be strong. A ruler must be strict and harsh because people are naturally evil. We can't help it. The dark side of human nature leads us. Rulers must be all-powerful to keep people from doing evil.

**PRINCE:** Just because I'm smart and work hard doesn't mean that I'm weak. I'm strong, very strong. And harsh. Anyone will tell you that. And strict. Ask anyone.

**TAOIST SCHOLAR:** All this arguing, my dear friends, is unnecessary—just as strict government is. People are neither good nor evil, and the world cannot be changed by people's actions. Nature determines what happens in the world. If people live in harmony with nature, then they will find true happiness. They will not need rulers.

**CONFUCIAN SCHOLAR:** But the population of China continues to grow and grow. The princes fight among themselves and invade other people's territories. We must have rules to tell everyone, from the emperor to the poorest of the poor, how to behave. We begin with the five different kinds of relationships: ruler and ruled, husband and wife, parents and children, older and younger brothers, and friends.

**PRINCE:** Here we go again. The rules set out for your family will not work with *my* family. We are natural leaders. We don't think—we do. We prefer action.

**TAOIST SCHOLAR:** But you don't consider the consequences of those actions.

**PRINCE:** Why should I?

**LEGALIST SCHOLAR:** All this talking around and around is very boring. Strict laws are the key. Let me tell you a story that will explain everything. Once there was a farmer. A tree stump sat right in the middle of his field. He plowed around it. One day, a hare ran out of the woods, ran right into the stump, broke its neck, and died. The farmer decided to leave his plow in the field to watch the stump. He thought that would prevent other hares from dying. What happened? Weeds took over the field. The farmer had no crops to sell or eat. He became poor. Here is my message: Rulers who abandon the laws to protect their people, as a father would, are foolish and will suffer for it!

**TAOIST SCHOLAR:** You are so wrong. A kind emperor will save people from hunger and all want. Strong emotions will be curbed. And all of this can be accomplished by following just a few rules.

**PRINCE:** You Taoists (*DOW-ists*) have your heads in the clouds. If everyone in China followed your path, the barbarians would take us over in no time!

**CONFUCIAN SCHOLAR:** Now let me tell you a story: One day Confucius passed a woman who was crying. When Confucius asked her what was wrong, she said that her husband's father had been killed here by a tiger, and so had her husband, and her son, all at different times. Confucius asked the woman why she didn't move. She answered that there was no oppressive government where she had chosen to live, only tigers. "Remember this, my children," said Confucius, "oppressive government is fiercer and more feared than a tiger."

**LEGALIST SCHOLAR:** Exactly, as it should be.

**PRINCE:** *I* am fiercer and more feared than a tiger, in addition to being smart and harsh and strict and hardworking and, of course, being a natural leader.

**TAOIST SCHOLAR:** Just be careful that the tiger doesn't eat you.

*(The Prince strides off.)*

**TAOIST SCHOLAR:** We are all one, but he doesn't see that. He sees only himself.

**CONFUCIAN SCHOLAR:** One must be able to obey commands as well as give them.

**LEGALIST SCHOLAR:** He is strict and harsh. Too bad he doesn't realize he's not the one who's making the rules.

# "SCHOOLS OF THOUGHT IN CHINA"

## DISCUSSION QUESTIONS

- Why do you think so many different ideas on how to govern were circulating at the end of the Zhou Dynasty?
- Which position from the play comes closest to representing your own viewpoint? Which positions are most difficult for you to understand?

## ACTIVITIES

### CONFUCIUS SAYS . . .

Encourage students to become experts on at least one of the major Chinese schools of thought (Confucianism, Taoism, Buddhism, Legalism, and so on) from this period. Divide the class into teams that specialize in a particular philosophy. Then present the class with problems generated from various sections of the newspaper: political, personal, or social. Have each group present how they would solve that problem according to their school's viewpoint. The discussion should highlight the contrasts between the different perspectives on responsibility, rules, and personal and spiritual values.

### I'M TELLING THE TRUTH!

Use the following activity to check students' understanding of the unique viewpoints held by each school of thought: Create a list of statements that supporters of each school might have said (perhaps inspired by lines from this script). Select a panel of four students, one to represent each philosophy. Present a statement from the list to the class and then ask each panel member to justify the statement with ideas from the philosophy he or she represents. The class must decide which argument best supports the statement—in other words, which panel member is "telling the truth!" Choose new students for the panel after each round so everyone has a chance to present an argument.

### DYNASTIES OVER TIME: CHARACTERISTICS AND ACHIEVEMENTS

To familiarize students with Chinese history, assign students individually or in groups to develop chronological charts with the following categories: Dynasty; Dates; Technology; Art; Religion and Philosophy; and Important Leaders. As individuals or groups learn about each dynasty, they fill in the chart, compiling information that will make an excellent resource and study guide. You may want to add additional categories and develop a large class chart on butcher paper.

## RESOURCES

### BOOKS

*China: A History to 1949* by Valjean McLenighan (Children's Press, 1983)

*Confucianism* by Thomas Hoobler, Dorothy Hoobler, and Francis X. Clooney (Facts on File, 1993)

*Made in China: Ideas and Inventions From Ancient China (Dragon Books)* by Suzanne Williams (Pacific View Press, 1997).

*Science in Ancient China* by George Beshore (Franklin Watts, Inc., 1998)

### WEBSITE

History of China (www-chaos.umd.edu/history/welcome.html)
Provides a useful time line, resource list, and outline of Chinese history, with visuals, covering all dynasties.

# THE Q'IN DYNASTY

## CHARACTERS

Narrator    Cheng (Shi Huangdi)    Adviser    Governor
Defender    Administrator    Noble    Li Si

**NARRATOR:** In a war that lasted more than a century and claimed millions of Chinese lives, the feudal state of Q'in defeated the last Zhou ruler in 256 BC A young man named Cheng became king. Within 25 years, he ruled all of China.

**CHENG:** A man with such power as mine deserves a powerful title. "Wang" or king is not good enough! I need a new title! Quickly!

**ADVISER:** May I suggest Shi Huangdi (*SHIR-HWHANG-DI*)?

**CHENG:** Shi Huangdi? Why? Give me one good reason.

**ADVISER:** It means "first emperor." This would suggest your family will rule for many, many years.

**CHENG:** It also means that there were no emperors before me. The history of China begins with me. I like it. You may call me Shi Huangdi from now on.

**NARRATOR:** Shi Huangdi knew that a strong title was not enough. The warring states of his empire had to be unified. He divided the empire into 36 provinces, and each of the provinces into districts.

**GOVERNOR:** What an excellent job we have. We rule the province together. What power!

**DEFENDER:** You bet!

**GOVERNOR:** What an excellent idea the emperor had—having his subjects spy on their neighbors and turn in anyone who breaks the law. Excellent idea. Now the Emperor has complete and total control over his Empire.

**DEFENDER:** You bet!

**NARRATOR:** Shi Huangdi's efforts to unify China didn't stop there. He set up a bureaucracy where workers were appointed and trained for specific jobs within the government. Not only that, the Emperor established new standards of measurement, a unified currency, and a set of written characters for all Chinese to use.

Scholastic Professional Books, 2000

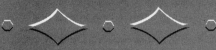

**ADMINISTRATOR:** Man, oh man, I get used to one thing and the Emperor comes along and changes everything! Now only one kind of money is legal in China. Now I have to learn a whole new way of writing. "One language," he says. "One kind of money." Easy for him to say. *(Looks around and then confides)* However, I will say this for the guy, he's made it easier for people to get around China. Very smart idea, making all cart axles the same size. Now every cart fits the ruts in our roads!

**NARRATOR:** Other people were angered by the Emperor's changes, too. Shi Huangdi abolished the feudal system of the Zhou Dynasty. The nobles hated this idea—they lost their land and their titles.

**NOBLE:** Just who does he think he is? First Emperor—hah! He can't take away my land. I served my lord for years and watched over those peasants. Did they ever say "Thank you"? They did not. Now First Emperor says anybody who can pay the tax can own the land. He'll see. The whole thing will blow up in his First-Emperor face.

**NARRATOR:** But Shi Huangdi wasn't finished yet. Li Si, one of his advisers, suggested another way the Emperor could strengthen control of his empire.

**LI SI:** Here's what I'm thinking. We burn all the books that don't support Legalism and your way of ruling. Then the people won't be able to learn anything we don't want them to learn—The teachings of Confucius, for example. They put such crazy ideas into the minds of our good and loyal citizens. Confucius confuses them.

**SHI HUANGDI:** A brilliant idea! I love censorship! It gives me such control! Build fires quickly! I want to burn books!

**NARRATOR:** Many of those punished were sent to work on a building project that the Emperor conceived to further unify his Empire. A crew of 300,000 men built a wall through northern China. The wall was designed to keep in the peasants and keep out invaders. This massive structure, more than 3,700 feet (5,960 km) long, is called the Great Wall of China and can even be seen from outer space. Many men died building it, but the unfinished wall never really succeeded in doing what it was supposed to do. Still, Shi Huangdi did unify his empire—often cruelly, but always shrewdly.

# "THE Q'IN DYNASTY"

## DISCUSSION QUESTIONS

- Do you agree with the policies Q'in Shi Huangdi used to expand and unify his empire?
- Do great achievements always require harsh policies and great hardship for many people?

## ACTIVITIES

### IMPERIAL STRATEGIST WANTED

As students study the sometimes awe-inspiring achievements of Q'in Shi Huangdi, encourage them to try to understand the rigid policies that made these achievements possible. Challenge students to assume the role of Shi Huangdi's adviser, Li Si, and compose a diary page outlining the imperial goals Li Si and the Emperor have conceived and the strategies they employ to achieve these goals. Students may find it helpful to organize their ideas on a T-chart, with goals like "imperial unification" on one side, and strategies on the other. Discuss the work students have done and ask them to consider alternative ways Shi Huangdi might have achieved some of these goals. What might he have had to sacrifice with less brutal policies?

### THE CENSORSHIP DEBATE

Censorship was a hot topic in the ancient China of Q'in Shi Huangdi and it continues to be a newsworthy subject today. Conduct a class debate about the advantages and disadvantages of censorship in ancient times and in American society today. Pull censorship examples from current headline topics that your students will relate to, such as music lyrics, television, video games, the V-chip, the Internet, and so on. The material and ideas your students generate can be used effectively in a lesson on persuasive writing or speaking.

### JUST HOW LONG IS THAT WALL?

Students are often fascinated by the Great Wall of Q'in Shi Huangdi. Encourage students to get a sense of the magnitude of this ancient building project by comparing it to distances they may have traveled. Refer students to United States or other relevant maps and have them use the scale to trace a cross-country route approximately 3,000 miles long. How many states will they cross? Will they be able to travel on land in a straight line?

## RESOURCES

### BOOKS

*Ancient China (See Through History* series) by Brian Willams (Viking Children's, 1996)
*The Great Wall (The Wonders of the World* series) by Elizabeth Mann (Mikaya, 1997)
*The Great Wall of China* by Leonard Everett Fisher (Aladdin, 1995)

# A TALE OF TWO CHINAS

## CHARACTERS
**Narrator 1    Narrator 2    City Chan    Country Chan**

**NARRATOR 1:** Once upon a time, in a dynasty long, long ago—

**NARRATOR 2:** Actually, it was the Han Dynasty, not so long ago. The Han rulers were in power from 206 to 220 BC, so it's only a little over 2,000 years ago.

**NARRATOR 1:** Thanks *so much* for clearing that up. As I was saying, a little over 2,000 years ago, there was a wealthy Chinese man named Chan who lived in the city. Like everyone, his life was filled with the wonders of the city—

**NARRATOR 2:** Actually, poor people in the city lived very differently than the wealthy did. Their houses were packed so closely together that there was barely room to breathe. And gangs terrorized the poor sections of the city, too.

**NARRATOR 1:** Thanks *so much*—again! Now, where was I?

**CITY CHAN:** It's my story. I'll tell it. I was very, very happy with my life. My house was very large and very beautiful. It had a courtyard in the middle filled with flowers and exotic birds. Inside the house were the finest rugs and draperies. And you should have seen my luxurious robes (silk or fox, sometimes both). My carriage was too elegant. I would take it to the center of the city to see the musicians, jugglers, and acrobats. I was very content with my life.

**NARRATOR 2:** Excuse me, City Chan, but don't you have a cousin who lives in the country? Didn't that cousin invite you—

**COUNTRY CHAN:** Yes, I did. I wrote my city cousin a letter that said: "Dear Cousin, I would like to invite you to visit my humble village. I haven't seen you in many years, and I would enjoy hearing what your life in the city is like. Very sincerely, Your Country Cousin."

**CITY CHAN:** Well, I rented an oxcart immediately and set off for my cousin's village. We always had a good time together when we were young.

**NARRATOR 1:** Chinese farmers who lived in the country lived very plainly and worked very hard.

**NARRATOR 2:** Boy, was City Chan in for a shock! No acrobats, no silk robes—

Scholastic Professional Books, 2000

*(City Chan and Country Chan greet each other.)*

**COUNTRY CHAN:** Welcome, Cousin! You're just in time for lunch. Come in and have some rice. We have a little fish, too. I caught it just this morning.

**CITY CHAN:** Oh, my. Is—is this your house? Mud walls and a thatched-straw roof? But where is your courtyard?

**COUNTRY CHAN:** No courtyards here, Cousin. We live close together with several other families to work the fields. We share whatever profits we make. My life here is simple, but it's a good life. I have all the fresh air I can breathe. There aren't any gangs or dirty streets.

**CITY CHAN:** This is really all we're having for lunch? A little rice and a little fish? No dumplings? No soup? Surely we must have some wine.

**COUNTRY CHAN:** This is all there is, Cousin. It's enough to fill your stomach and give you strength to plow a field.

**CITY CHAN:** Give *me* strength to plow a field?

**COUNTRY CHAN:** After lunch, we'll help water the fields. It takes every man, woman, and child in the village to carry enough water to the crops. I hope you brought other clothing, Cousin. That fox robe will be too heavy to work in. Those leather slippers are beautiful, but the fields are wet and muddy; they'll be ruined.

**CITY CHAN:** But where are your oxen and your plows?

**COUNTRY CHAN:** Those things cost money, which I don't have.

**CITY CHAN:** Cousin, it has truly been a joy to see you again, but I really must get back to the city. Country life doesn't agree with me. I need to be fed well and entertained. Come and visit me sometime in the city.

**COUNTRY CHAN:** Maybe we should just write to each other and tell about our lives.

**CITY CHAN:** Good idea, Cousin!

**NARRATOR 1:** And with that, City Chan boarded his cart and went back to the city. Country Chan finished his small meal and then returned to work in the field.

**NARRATOR 2:** Whew, there were big differences in the lifestyles of the Chinese people during the Han Dynasty, weren't there?

**NARRATOR 1:** You had to have the last word, didn't you?

**NARRATOR 2:** Oops! Sorry.

# "A TALE OF TWO CHINAS"

## DISCUSSION QUESTIONS

• Why do you think there were such drastic differences in the quality of life between the wealthy urban merchant class and the poor rural farmers during this period?

• What are some status symbols in American society today? Why do you think people display status symbols?

## ACTIVITIES

### SOCIAL ORDER-ING

After students have read about the social hierarchy in ancient China, have them sketch a diagram to show the status of groups like the merchants, scholar-officials, soldiers, women, and slaves. Use the diagrams to discuss the divisions that existed among the classes and to what extent the classes were fixed or flexible. Students who have studied the caste system in India should be able to compare and contrast it with the Chinese social hierarchy.

### THIS OLD FOLKTALE

Folktales that feature ordinary people can provide students with evidence about daily life long ago. Charge students with locating and selecting a folktale with roots in ancient China. Encourage them to write a diary page describing a particular character's point of view. As students share these fictional accounts, they develop a sense of what daily life was like for people in the lower classes and how lives differed across regions.

### NOT AGAIN!—DYNASTIC CYCLES

Some historians claim that the rise and fall of dynasties from ancient to modern times has followed a pattern called "the dynastic cycle." Encourage students to research this phenomenon and label the parts of the cycle (e.g., Rise of the Dynasty, Peace and Prosperity, Decline) on a circular chart (a paper plate works well). Extend the activity by asking students to apply the cycle model to a particular dynasty. Students may compare dynasties and whether they fit the pattern. The chart should include possible causes for each stage and effects.

## RESOURCES

### BOOKS

*Ancient China (Eyewitness Books)* by Arthur Cotterell (Knopf, 1994)

*The Chin-Lin Purse: A Collection of Ancient Chinese Stories* by Linda Fang (Straus & Giroux Juveniles, 1994)

*Growing Up in Ancient China* by Ken Teague (Troll Association, 1993)

*Weaving of a Dream: A Chinese Folktale (Picture Puffins)* by Marilee Heyer (Viking, 1989)

# TO THE WEST: THE AMERICAS

## SETTING THE STAGE: MINI-PLAY 17

Section IV features the Olmec civilization, which developed during the first millennium in ancient America. The Olmecs made many contributions in math, science, writing, sculpture, and architecture—all in isolation from the rest of the ancient world. Recently, archaeologists have dubbed the Olmecs the "parent culture" of Central American civilization, a distinction previously given to the Maya (c. 250–900 AD).

## BACKGROUND

Olmec civilization, like most other civilizations, did not just spring up in an ideal location. Archaeologists believe that Ice Age hunter-gatherers, in search of warmer climates and more plentiful food sources, migrated over a land bridge from Asia or Africa to the Americas. Agriculturally based communities began to settle around coastal regions in southern Mexico and Central America sometime between 9000 and 6000 BC. By about 1200 BC, the Olmec civilization began to flourish, developing a strong, agricultural base and exploiting local natural resources, like rubber and volcanic rock.

In **"The Olmecs,"** two American students discover some of the impressive achievements of this ancient culture, including the development of an advanced mathematics that used the concept of zero long before mathematicians in India did. The characters also learn that religion played a central role in daily life and that priests are believed to have held positions of authority. One of the priests' duties involved overseeing *pok-a-tok*, an important ritual game much like basketball. Priests also helped organize the sculpting and transportation of huge, 14-foot stone heads over many miles on log rollers.

# THE OLMECS

## CHARACTERS
**American students: Kim Acosta and Robert Luke,**
**Olmecs: Mathematician, Student, Priest, Worker, Player 1, Player 2**

---

**KIM:** Hey, Robert! I finally found a research topic! I'm doing my report on the Olmec people. They lived in Mexico more than 2,000 years ago. Their name means "rubber people."

**ROBERT:** Rubber people? No way! Why would anybody call themselves that?

**KIM:** *They* didn't call themselves Olmecs. That's what *we* call them. They were the first people to tap rubber trees for the sap. Then they turned the sap into rubber and used it to make stuff, like bouncing balls. And they figured out the idea of zero.

**ROBERT:** Doesn't everybody know about zero?

(*Enter Mathematician and Student.*)

**MATHEMATICIAN:** See, here's what I'm telling you. If I put these five mangos on the table, and then I take all of them away, what do I have?

**STUDENT:** You have those five mangos that you just took away.

**MATHEMATICIAN:** No! We have NOTHING! Zero! *Nada!* Don't you get it?

**STUDENT:** Well, I can still see those five mangos in your hands, and I'm getting kind of hungry. Can you hand me one? Then you'll have four. (*Exits with Mathematician*)

**KIM:** *And* they moved gigantic blocks of stone over 50 miles without using animals or wheels. They carved huge heads out of the stone. Some of the heads weighed 20 tons.

**ROBERT:** That's . . . wait a minute . . . 40,000 pounds! How'd they do it?

(*Enter Priest and Worker.*)

**PRIEST:** All right, workers! Let's move it out! I know it's heavy! I know it's big! I know we don't have wheels or animals to help us, but that's no excuse. This is important, so move that head!

**WORKER:** But how are we going to move this huge head one foot, much less 50 or 60 miles?

**PRIEST:** That's why we have these logs. We'll hoist the head onto the logs and use them as rollers to get us to the river. Then we'll slide it onto the raft and *voila!* We've got ourselves a head headed downstream.

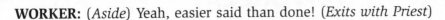

**WORKER:** (*Aside*) Yeah, easier said than done! (*Exits with Priest*)

**ROBERT:** You can't always believe everything you get off the Internet, you know.

**KIM:** True, but I found at least three sources for each fact. Here, this is cool: They played a game like basketball, only they called it *pok-a-tok*.

**ROBERT:** Oh, right. Like the Olmecs invented basketball! Explain *pok-a-whatever*.

**KIM:** You had to try to get a ball through a stone ring that stuck out of a high stone wall, BUT you couldn't use your hands, only your hips and your elbows. Plus, if the priests didn't like the way you played, they might sacrifice you to the gods.

*(Enter Player 1 and Player 2.)*

**PLAYER 1:** Hey, I'm playing again today—I hope I can get the ball through the ring at least once! You know they sacrificed that player who didn't score last time.

**PLAYER 2:** Yeah, just make sure you don't cheat like you usually do. You'll be the next ex-player the way you keep using your hands. (*Exits with Player 1*)

**ROBERT:** No way! They'd never get away with penalties like that in the NBA!

**KIM:** No kidding. But there's more: The Olmecs studied the planets and recorded their orbits, and they predicted eclipses. They also built these cool structures shaped like volcanoes and set temples right on top.

**ROBERT:** Sounds like they stole that idea from the Egyptians. Sounds like a pyramid to me.

**KIM:** A: they didn't bury their kings in the temples, like the Egyptians did. B: the Olmecs didn't even know the Egyptians existed, and vice versa.

**ROBERT:** Yeah, that's what they say now.

**KIM:** No, they don't. There aren't any Olmecs left. They disappeared in the 1st century BC, and nobody knows what happened.

**ROBERT:** Too bad. They sure sounded interesting.

**KIM:** Well, they did influence other American cultures like the Maya and the Aztecs.

**ROBERT:** So the Olmecs were kind of like the parents of the other cultures of the Americas?

**KIM:** Exactly!

**ROBERT:** Cool. Since I'm practically an Olmecs expert now, I think I'm going to do my report on them, too.

**KIM:** No way!

# "THE OLMECS"

## DISCUSSION QUESTIONS

- Describe three differences between *pok-a-tok* and basketball.
- Since experts still have not decoded Olmec hieroglyphic writing, how have they been able to discover so much about this civilization?

## ACTIVITIES

### READY, SET, PLAY!

Encourage students to research the *pok-a-tok* ritual. In pairs or small groups, students can develop a set of rules for playing this game and make a poster explaining them. Have students include sketches that detail the rules and violations. As an extension, students may want to go outdoors and try playing their version of the game. Ask them to consider what kind of ball would come closest to the Olmec's rubber ball and what could serve as a ring through which to send the ball. Discuss what rules students had to invent themselves and the ways in which their "game" differed from *pok-a-tok*.

### A COLOSSAL JOB

Conduct a study of the stone heads found at Olmec sites. Have the class outline distinguishing characteristics, such as the size, shape, and style of the heads, as an archaeologist would. Then discuss what type of rituals might have been associated with these heads and what kind of jobs or activities would have been necessary to produce and transport ritual objects this size.

### MAIZE AND MORE!

Invite students to design a pamphlet which describes and illustrates the types of plants the Olmecs may have cultivated and the farming techniques they may have used, including *chinampas*, or floating gardens. Ask students how information has been gathered on Olmec farming when no written records can be deciphered.

## RESOURCES

### BOOKS

*Ancient America (Cultural Atlas for Young People* series*)* by Marion Wood (Chekmark Books, 1990)

*Mexico: From the Olmecs to the Aztecs* by Michael D. Coe (Thames & Hudson, 1994)

*Science of the Early Americas (Science of the Past)* by Geraldine Woods (Franklin Watts, Inc., 1999)

### WEBSITE

Behind the Art: Mexico's Lost Civilizations
(www.nationalgeographic.com/ngm/9608/bts/a060.html)
Article with Olmec art images from *National Geographic Magazine On-Line,* August 1996.

# GREECE

## SETTING THE STAGE: MINI-PLAYS 18, 19, 20, AND 21

The four plays in this section feature Greece in the Classical Era. Mini-plays 19 and 20 highlight the cultural achievements of the Greeks and the important political institutions that continue to be models for democratic nations today. Mini-plays 18 and 21 illustrate how military strength and strategies helped keep Greece independent of Persian control, and how Macedonian leader Alexander the Great encouraged the beginning of the Hellenistic Age with his admiration for Greek culture.

## BACKGROUND

The seafaring Greeks were united by an extensive trade network and a rich culture consisting of a common religion and language, Homer's epics, and the Olympic games. Around the beginning of the Hellenic Age (c. 800 BC), the Greek city-state, or polis, emerged as a religious, political, and military center.

Despite their diverse outlooks and forms of government, the Greek city-states united to form an alliance that would repel powerful Persian invaders. With each polis contributing ships, soldiers, and money to the Delian League, the Greeks—led by the major city-states Athens and Sparta—

repelled the Persians from Aegean shores repeatedly between 490 and 479. **"Victory at Marathon"** highlights the first major victory of the Persian Wars. It describes a crucial battle in which the small Athenian army defeated a much larger but demoralized Persian force. By the end of the war, the Greeks were free of Persian domination.

One result of the Greek victory was the continued development of democracy in Athens. Since the middle of the 6th century, reformers had expanded the role of citizens of all classes, with the notable exception of slaves and women. All full citizens—free men whose parents were both Athenian—participated in the political life of the polis by voting, serving as jury members, and working as statesmen. Under the leadership of Pericles (640-429 BC), Athenian citizens enjoyed the greatest levels of firsthand involvement in a direct democracy. **"A Trial in Athens"** illustrates how a trial would have proceeded during the Golden Age of democracy in Athens.

Widespread disease and destruction from the 27–year Peloponnesian War (431–404 BC) weakened the city-states and cast doubts in the minds of citizens regarding religion and government. In Athens, the disaffected social climate set the stage for the rise of new philosophies, which sought to uncover "basic truths" of life. The third play, **"Socrates,"** presents the famous philosopher who challenged the young men of Athens to question their assumptions and consider how they should live their lives. Conservative politicians capitalized on Socrates' unpopular views and pegged him as an antiestablishment target. In 399 BC, Socrates was brought to trial, convicted, and given the death sentence for corrupting the youth of Athens and for his religious views, which differed from those of the state.

Into the Greek power vacuum stepped leaders from Macedonia, a kingdom to the north of the Greek peninsula. In 338 BC, King Philip and his army descended upon and conquered the quarrelling city-states. Though the Greeks lost their independence, the Macedonian leadership was heavily influenced by Greek culture. Philip's son, Alexander, featured in the fourth play, studied under the renowned Greek philosophers Aristotle and Ptolemy and modeled himself after Homer's epic heroes. **"Alexander the Great"** highlights the military prowess of this important leader and shows how his appreciation of Greek culture ushered in the Hellenistic Age throughout the Mediterranean. Many aspects of ancient Greek heritage continue to serve as models and subjects of study for modern societies, particularly in western Europe and the United States.

# VICTORY AT MARATHON

## CHARACTERS
**Atticus    Calista    Persian General**
**Persian Messenger    Phidippides    Greek Messenger    Miltiades**

**ATTICUS:** This is Atticus, your roving reporter, on the scene in Marathon. Six hundred Persian ships sit in the harbor. Persian forces have landed here, just 25 miles away from Athens. Apparently, King Darius hasn't forgiven Athens for helping the Greek colonists in Persia revolt against him just nine years ago in 499 BC. Let's go to Calista, who's with the one of the Persian generals.

**CALISTA:** Well, you're absolutely right, Atticus. I'm here with a Persian general, who says that Darius is still spitting mad about the Greek colonists burning down the Lydian capital of Sardis nine years ago. He's especially mad at Athens for sending 20 ships to help the Greek colonists.

**PERSIAN GENERAL:** I wouldn't say that.

**CALISTA:** Well, don't you think the Persian Empire is big enough? Does Darius really plan to take over Greece? Isn't he having a tough time already ruling such a vast amount of territory with so many different groups of people in it?

**PERSIAN GENERAL:** I wouldn't say that.

**CALISTA:** Well, what would you say?

**PERSIAN GENERAL:** All the Greek people would be united under Darius's rule. Look at the situation now. The Greek city-states have fought each other for years. Athenians don't like Spartans because they have a military government and train their children to be warriors. Spartans don't like Athenians because they focus too much on developing the mind and have political freedom.

**CALISTA:** Well, I'm willing to bet the Athenians like Spartans better than they like Persians.

**PERSIAN GENERAL:** I wouldn't say that.

*(A Persian messenger rushes in and whispers in the General's ear.)*

**CALISTA:** What's going on, general? What can you tell me? General? General?

*(The Persian General rushes off with the messenger.)*

**CALISTA:** Back to you, Atticus.

**ATTICUS:** Thanks, Calista. I've managed to track down Phidippides (*fih-DIP-uh-deez*), probably the fastest runner in all of Greece. He's just back from Sparta. When can we expect the Spartan army to arrive? That's okay, catch your breath, buddy. I'd be breathing hard too, if I'd been running for two straight days.

**PHIDIPPIDES:** *(Breathing heavily)* Next full moon. Celebrating religious festival.

**ATTICUS:** Oh, that's bad news. The Athenian army numbers in the hundreds, but the Persian army numbers in the thousands—wait a minute, folks! Something's happening! Miltiades (*mil-TY-uh-deez*) is leading the Greek army against the Persians! Oh my! The Persians are pushing back the center of the Greek army! But wait! The two outside wings of the Greek army are meeting behind the Persians! Yes! Yes! The Persians are trapped! Miltiades has done it! He's stopped the Persians!

*(A Greek messenger rushes in and whispers in Phidippides' ear.)*

**PHIDIPPIDES:** *(Breathing heavily)* Gotta run. Gotta spread the good news in Athens.

**ATTICUS:** Miltiades! Miltiades! Over here! Can I have a few words?

**MILTIADES:** It'll have to be quick, Atticus. I have to tour the battlefield and make sure the wounded are tended to. It looks like they suffered more than 6,000 casualties. We lost almost 200 men.

**ATTICUS:** That was a brilliant strategy out there.

**MILTIADES:** I knew we couldn't wait for the Spartans to arrive, so we had to act fast. I kept the center weak and built up the outside wings. We were able to surround the Persians. Their bows and arrows were no match for our spears.

*(The Greek messenger rushes in again and whispers in Miltiades' ear.)*

**ATTICUS:** Looks like bad news, folks. What is it, Miltiades?

**MILTIADES:** It's Phidippides. He made it to Athens and then collapsed. Just before he died he delivered his message: "Rejoice! We conquer!" . . . . I must go.

*(Miltiades hurries off.)*

**ATTICUS:** There you have it, folks. A sad note on a happy day.

# "VICTORY AT MARATHON"

## DISCUSSION QUESTIONS

- Why do you think Darius might have wanted to conquer Greece? What was so important about adding the city-states to the Persian Empire?
- Describe the Greek communication system.

## ACTIVITIES

### WHERE DID THAT WORD COME FROM?

Help students understand that many common words today originated in ancient Greece, such as *atlas, marathon,* and *amazon*. Challenge your students to find more words of Greek origin and create short skits that illustrate how these words came into English.

### DARIUS' PROMISE

Invite students to imagine they are Darius' top military leaders receiving his orders before the battle at Marathon. What tone would Darius have used? What reasons might he have given for overtaking the Greeks? What might this successful conqueror have said about the much smaller Greek force? Have students write a diary page that captures the reactions of a general taking orders from Darius. Nonfiction sources on the Persian forces (see page 38) and on the Battle of Marathon should help supply important details.

### ATHENS AND SPARTA: BOTH GREEK?

The ancient Athenians and Spartans had such different political and social institutions that it's sometimes hard to believe both societies were Greek. Invite students to appreciate the differences and similarities between Athenians and Spartans by dividing the class into two "Greek" groups. Each side must study the group it represents (Athenian or Spartan) to prepare for questions or criticisms from the other side. Within the groups each student should be responsible for at least one question aimed at the other side on issues, such as social organization; the position of metics, women, slaves, foreigners, and people with disabilities; religion; personal responsibility; education; and participation in government. You might organize the discussion as a debate and assign topics or questions for each team to respond to in a given period of time.

## RESOURCES

### BOOKS

*Ancient Greece (Eyewitness Books)* by Anne Pearson (Knopf, 1992)
*Greek Myths: 8 Short Plays for the Classroom* by John Rearick (Scholastic Professional Books, 1997)

### WEBSITES

The Quiz Site (www.quizsite.com/quiz/history)
   Click on "Ancient Greece" to find an interactive quiz on the Persian Wars.
Daily Life in Ancient Greece (www.members.aol.com/DonnClass/Greeklife.html)
   Site developed by middle school history teachers on Athens, Sparta, Corinth, Argos, and Megara.

# A TRIAL IN ATHENS

## CHARACTERS

**Narrator    Survivor    Mourner    General    Public Crier**

---

**NARRATOR:** The year is 406 BC in Athens. This trial is turning out to be the most exciting and important that Athenians have heard this year. A jury of 200 citizens— free men whose parents are both Athenians—is ready to decide the fate of six navy generals. The generals are charged with abandoning hundreds of soldiers at sea and leaving them to drown.

**SURVIVOR:** I was on a ship that went down that day. I watched those six cowards— excuse me, generals—save themselves. We were pleading with them to stay with us, to help us, to *save* us! I was able to grab hold of a flour barrel and float to safety. I floated for days and days, and my only thought was that I had to live to tell the true story of what happened that day. Those six men are guilty of abandoning us and failing to fulfill their duty as officers! Convict them!

**MOURNER:** Oh, the horrible loss!

**NARRATOR:** All through the trial, men dressed in black circulate among the crowd. These are professional mourners—men paid to wail and cry and try to convince the jury to convict the generals. (Did I mention that jurors are paid to serve?)

**MOURNER:** So many men have died! Oh, mighty Zeus! Punish the evil men who are responsible for the deaths of so many! So tragic! Such despair!

**NARRATOR:** Now it's the defendants' turn. Each man can speak as long as the water clock allows. What? You don't know what a water clock is? Well then, I guess I'll have to tell you. A water clock is made of two urns . . . like big clay vases. Water is poured into the upper urn and then empties into the lower urn. When the upper urn is empty, the speaker's time is up. Simple. Ssh! Here comes the first general.

**GENERAL:** Good and wise citizens of Athens, please consider the facts. Neither I nor my colleagues are guilty of any wrongdoing. Of course I tried to save my men from drowning! What man in his right mind would let someone drown? But circumstances were beyond my—our—control. Fate dictated that those poor souls would die a most unfortunate death. I did what I could, you understand, but fate was against me—us.

Scholastic Professional Books, 2000

**MOURNER:** Liar! Scoundrel! Coward!

**NARRATOR:** The other five generals say the same thing when they come to the stand. Each one claims he is innocent of any crime; he was simply helpless on that day and unable to save so many men. (Did I mention that Athenian courts don't have any judges or lawyers?)

**SURVIVOR:** *(Shouting)* You're here to testify for yourselves—my crewmates aren't! They're at the bottom of the sea, thanks to you! Not one of you *generals* went to the bottom of the sea with them, did you?

**NARRATOR:** Now it's time for the jury to decide whether the generals are guilty or innocent.

**PUBLIC CRIER:** Listen up! Every man who thinks the generals are guilty of deserting their men and letting them drown, put the bronze token with the hole in it in this urn. Every man who thinks the generals are innocent, put the solid bronze token in this urn. If all six generals are found guilty, the penalty will be . . . death.

**SURVIVOR:** Give them what they deserve! Give them death!

**MOURNER:** Think of the mothers and fathers who have lost their sons! Think of the sons and daughters! Think of the wives and sisters! Oh, the tragedy of it!

**NARRATOR:** Okay, all 200 jurors have cast their votes. Now four different men are counting the tokens in each urn. Looks like they'll announce the verdict soon.

**PUBLIC CRIER:** Listen up! All six generals have been found guilty as charged! The sentence is death!

**SURVIVOR:** Justice!

**GENERAL:** No! I'm innocent! I can't speak for the others, but I AM INNOCENT! You have to listen to me!

**PUBLIC CRIER:** That's enough of that. You've had your say, and you've been judged.

**NARRATOR:** Whew, that was some trial. As you can see, citizens in Athens are directly involved in the government. (Did I mention that women and slaves in Athens aren't citizens?) Athenian citizens not only serve on juries but also vote for leaders and laws in the Assembly, a model for government that the authors of the United States Constitution will emulate in the future.

Scholastic Professional Books, 2000

# "A TRIAL IN ATHENS"

## DISCUSSION QUESTIONS

- Do you think the sentence of the defendants in this trial was fair? What is your position on making crimes punishable by death?
- How direct was Athenian democracy (who was included and who was excluded)? Think of groups or organizations in your school and community that have governments in which you do or can participate directly. What are the rules about who can participate and why are those rules in place?

## ACTIVITIES

### STATE YOUR CASE

What are the differences between a democratic trial in 7th century Athens and one in our country today? Have students compare **"A Trial in Athens"** with a live or televised criminal court case. Invite students to take notes on the similarities and differences they notice. Create a class chart that compares the procedures of the trial as well as the roles, responsibilities, and numbers of the participants involved. Discuss the impact of the two forms of democracy—direct and representative—on the participation of citizens in government.

### THE HEARTBEAT OF DEMOCRACY

An imitation line graph of peaks and troughs can help students trace and evaluate the development of democracy in Athens. On the x-axis, students may place, in chronological order, events such as the rule of archons, the laws of Draco, the reforms of Solon, the rule of Pisistratus, Cleisthenes' reforms, Pericles' reforms, and the end of the Peloponnesian War. On the y-axis, students should decide on an ultimate peak for direct democracy. They may plot points above each event to show how close to or far from direct democracy the resolution of the event comes. When students connect the points, their evaluation should resemble a line graph. Ask students to compare their "graphs" and use their analyses to discuss whether or not Athens ever achieved a direct democracy.

### MAP-A-GOVERNMENT

Encourage your students to design a political map of Greece that shows the different forms of government developed by each city-state after 800 BC. Students may use colors, symbols, or shading to distinguish the governments. Challenge students to write definitions for political terms, such as monarchy and democracy, and important notes about the city-state governments on index cards marked to correspond to map symbols or colors. Students can arrange these artfully around the border for an attractive display.

## RESOURCES

### BOOKS

*The Ancient City: Life in Classical Athens and Rome* by Peter Connolly and Hazel Dodge (Oxford University Press, 1998)

*Athens (Cities of the World)* by Richard Conrad Stein (Children's Press, 1997)

*Growing up in Ancient Greece* by Chris Chelepi (Troll, 1992)

## CHARACTERS

**Narrator     Sophist     Student     Socrates     Antyus     Meletus     Plato**

*Scene 1: Athens street corner, 432 BC*

**NARRATOR:** With the end of the Peloponnesian War, Athens became quite turbulent. Democracy no longer united the city. In fact, many younger citizens refused to take part in public affairs. Sophists *(SAHF-ists)* tried to change this by teaching young people debating and other political skills—for a fee. The philosopher Socrates, however, shared his wisdom for free.

**SOPHIST:** Uh-oh, here comes Socrates. Don't turn around! Maybe he won't see us.

**STUDENT:** Him? That barefoot man wearing rags? He's the wisest man in Athens?

**SOPHIST:** That's Socrates, all right, but he's not the wisest man in Athens—he only thinks he is.

**SOCRATES:** You! Sophist! Still taking money from people hoping you'll make them wise? You Sophists are nothing but crooks.

**STUDENT:** I don't mind paying to learn. Why, I can make an argument for or against almost anything now. I'll be able to really take part in governing Athens—

**SOCRATES:** But what do *you* believe in? Know thyself. How can you make an argument for something you don't believe in?

**STUDENT:** Well, sometimes there's more than one way to look at an argument.

**SOPHIST:** Don't waste your breath. Socrates doesn't believe that ordinary citizens should take part in ruling themselves. He thinks that only one ruler should tell everybody else what to do, and citizens should do it.

**SOCRATES:** A wise ruler. *(Turning to student)* Tell me, why do you think you should participate in government?

**SOPHIST:** We'd *love* to talk, Socrates, but we've got a really important appointment. Later.

*Scene 2: House in Athens, 400 BC*

**NARRATOR:** Many pupils gathered around Socrates. Some Athenian leaders feared he was teaching young people to challenge the authority of the government.

**ANTYUS:** Athens is still in danger. We've survived Alcibiades' (*al-suh-BY-uh-deez*) betrayal of us to the Spartans. (And who was his teacher? Socrates.) We've survived the takeover by the Thirty Tyrants. (Did Socrates speak out against their tyranny? No.) We have democracy again, but we must protect it. We can't have Socrates running around saying that we citizens cannot rule ourselves.

**MELETUS:** But how can we stop him?

**ANTYUS:** By bringing charges against him. How about this: He doesn't worship the same gods that the state does. Second, he's a bad influence on the youth of Athens. He teaches them to disrespect their parents and the government. Yes, I like the sound of that. You'll bring those two charges against our "wise" philosopher.

**MELETUS:** Me!?! Why me? I'm just a poet. Who'll listen to me?

**ANTYUS:** I'm a politician, and a well-liked one, too. I don't want to give that up if Socrates is found innocent.

*Scene 3: Athens courtroom, 399 BC*

**NARRATOR:** Socrates was arrested and tried before a jury of Athenian citizens.

**PLATO:** I wish you'd left Athens when you had the chance, Socrates. That's what they wanted you to do. They don't really want you to stand trial and be convicted.

**SOCRATES:** I've been accused. I must stand trial and defend myself. Haven't I always spoken for upholding the rules of government?

**PLATO:** You have, but you've made a lot of people mad by proving that they're not as smart as they think they are. I see some of those people on the jury, too.

**SOCRATES:** There are 500 people on the jury. I only need to convince 250 of them of my innocence.

*(A few days later.)*

**PLATO:** They've sentenced you to death! How could they?

**SOCRATES:** Now we go our separate ways—I to die, and you to live . . . and teach. Good-bye, Plato. Good-bye, friends.

**PLATO:** I weep now, not for Socrates, but for myself and all of Athens, that we have lost such a good friend and teacher.

# "SOCRATES"

## DISCUSSION QUESTIONS

- What do you think Socrates meant when he said "Know thyself"? What did he want the student to think about?
- Do you think the method of questioning Socrates used was effective? Have you ever used a similar strategy to get someone to think about he or she was saying?

## ACTIVITIES

### IN DEFENSE OF SOCRATES

Invite students to write a letter from the perspective of one of Socrates' pupils that defends him. In their letters of defense, students should counter accusations from fellow Athenians that Socrates has corrupted the youth of Athens and that his religious views are anti-Greek. Students may want to write the letter in the form of a persuasive essay or invent a dialogue that uses the Socratic question-and-answer method (e.g., they might create an imaginary dialogue between themselves or Socrates and his accusers, in the style of Plato's writings). The letters can be posted and serve as a springboard for discussion.

### WHO'S WHO IN ANCIENT GREECE

Create a class Who's Who guide to familiarize students with important ancient Greeks and their contributions to Greek culture. Sections might include philosophy, literature, art and architecture, science, mathematics, politics, and so on. To develop a student-friendly resource, encourage student input about the format of the pages and how the resource should be arranged (chronologically, alphabetically, or otherwise). Collect the pages in a binder with dividers and a clear plastic cover to make an instant book.

### WALL OF GODS AND GODDESSES

Read aloud or assign students to read several Greek myths. Ask students to describe Greek gods and goddesses and their relationship to humans, explaining how this god-human relationship was different in other ancient cultures. Then students can develop a Wall of Gods and Goddesses. Give them the opportunity to illustrate and write an informative caption about the deities of their choice, and post their artwork. Alternatively, students might create an acrostic poem using the name of a god or goddess. Lining the images up in alphabetical order or arranging them to show the genealogy of the gods makes an excellent resource tool and an attractive display of student work.

## RESOURCES

### BOOKS

*Ancient Greece: Gods and Goddesses* by John Malam (Peter Bedrick, 1999)
*Ancient Greeks (Worldwise)* by Daisy Kerr (Franklin Watts, 1997)
*The Trial of Socrates* by Don Nardo (Lucent, 1997)

# ALEXANDER THE GREAT

## CHARACTERS

**Alexander    Aristotle    Philip    Ptolemy    Oracle    Soldiers 1–3**

*Scene 1: Macedonia in 343 BC. Alexander is 13 years old.*

**ALEXANDER:** But my father loves the Greeks. He brought you from Greece to teach me, didn't he? Why do they think we Macedonians *(mas-uh-DOH-nee-anz)* are barbarians?

**ARISTOTLE:** They're afraid of you. The city-states think your father will sweep in and take them over.

**ALEXANDER:** He should. They're always fighting one another. My father could bring them together.

**ARISTOTLE:** If he does, then it'll be your job one day to keep them together. Learn everything you can today—politics, ethics, botany, zoology, medicine, geography— a smart ruler is a good ruler.

*Scene 2: Chaeronea, Greece, in 338 BC. Alexander is 18 years old.*

**PHILIP:** Did you see Alexander leading the left wing, Ptolemy ? My son destroyed the Sacred Band of the Thebans!

**PTOLEMY:** Yes, sir, I did. He's a fine soldier.

**ALEXANDER:** All the city-states except Sparta have pledged their allegiance to you, Father. Greece is in our hands!

**PHILIP:** We're not done yet. I want Darius' Persian empire in my hands.

*Scene 3: Hellespont, 334 BC. Alexander is 22 years old.*

**PTOLEMY:** Philip would be proud of you. Today you lead a mighty army into Asia Minor.

**ALEXANDER:** It's hard to believe that it's been two years since my father was murdered. *(Pauses)* Everything's in order then?

**PTOLEMY:** Yes, sir. I've never heard of an army marching with a historian, a surveyor, a botanist, and a geographer before.

Scholastic Professional Books, 2000

*Scene 4: Gordium in Asia Minor, a few months later*

**ORACLE:** Legend has it that whoever can untie this knot will rule Asia. Many have tried before you, Alexander, but no one has succeeded.

**ALEXANDER:** I will.

*(The Oracle hands Alexander the Gordian knot. Alexander cuts it with his sword. The Oracle gasps and bows.)*

*Scene 5: Alexandria, Egypt, 332 BC. Alexander is 24 years old.*

**PTOLEMY:** The Egyptians are calling you their new pharaoh.

**ALEXANDER:** They're just glad to be rid of the Persians. Here, take a look at these plans, Ptolemy. Tell me what you think of my new city on the Nile—Alexandria.

**PTOLEMY:** Then you plan to stay here for a while?

**ALEXANDER:** No. I'm not stopping until I've met Darius on the battlefield. Then all of Asia Minor will be mine.

*Scene 6: Camel's House in Asia Minor in 331 BC. Alexander is 25 years old.*

**SOLDIER 1:** Did you see him? Did you see Alexander?

**SOLDIER 2:** Did I ever! He led the cavalry straight toward Darius!

**SOLDIER 3:** Darius turned tail and ran! There were chariots and elephants and men and horses everywhere! What a victory for Alexander!

*Scene 7: India, 327 BC. Alexander is 29 years old.*

**PTOLEMY:** Alexander, sir, your men have marched more than 11,000 miles. You've conquered Greece, Egypt, Babylon, all of Persia, and now India. The men can't go on much farther. And look at you—you've marched along with your men; you've been wounded how many times?

**ALEXANDER:** Very well, Ptolemy. We'll sail down the Indus and then march across the desert. Tell the men we're going home.

*Scene 8: Babylon in 323 BC. Alexander is 33 years old.*

**SOLDIER 1:** They say Alexander has the fever.

**SOLDIER 2:** Don't worry, he'll throw it off. He's been sick before.

**SOLDIER 3:** Hey, there's Ptolemy! General! How's—

**PTOLEMY:** Alexander the Great is dead. Mark this date—June 13. The greatest ruler the world has ever known has died.

# "ALEXANDER THE GREAT"

## DISCUSSION QUESTIONS

• What personal qualities or experiences helped Alexander build such a vast empire? What was happening in Greece that helped to make his empire building successful?
• What impact did Aristotle have on Alexander?

## ACTIVITIES

### ALEXANDER'S REQUIRED READING
After students have located and browsed through resources on Alexander the Great, challenge them to consider the following question: *If you were placed in Aristotle's position and had to tutor the future ruler of a vast empire, what lessons would you teach?* Have students create a daylong lesson plan that includes subjects to be studied and resources to be used.

### HOW TO LEAD AN EMPIRE
Help students make historical connections across cultures by encouraging them to compare Alexander's leadership style with that of another ruler. Students may want to select a ruler they have already studied from the Persian, Assyrian, or Egyptian empires. They can also pair up, divide the research, and compare notes on their subjects. A Venn diagram is useful for collecting and comparing data on the leaders.

### AN EMPIRE DIVIDED
When Alexander died, his successors could not manage to keep the huge empire united. Have students tackle a map that shows the maximum size of Alexander's empire, including all the areas under Macedonian control. Then have students use tracing paper or transparency film to demarcate where the empire split up after Alexander's death.

## RESOURCES

### BOOKS
*Alexander and His Times* by Fredric Theule (Henry Holt, 1996)
*The Children's Homer* by Padraic Colum (Aladdin, 1982). Young-adult level text, not for young children, as title suggests.
*The World in the Time of Alexander the Great* by Fiona MacDonald (Dillon Press, 1997)

# ROME

## SETTING THE STAGE: MINI-PLAYS 22, 23, 24, AND 25

The plays in this section cover the birth of Rome, from settlement to mighty empire. Mini-play 22 features Rome's founding myth, while mini-plays 23 and 24 highlight class struggle and military expansion during the years of the Roman Republic. Mini-play 25 concludes the section with the death of Rome's most powerful and popular dictator, Julius Caesar, and the dawn of the Roman Empire.

## BACKGROUND

**"Romulus and Remus"** recounts the legendary founding of Rome by Romulus, one of the twin sons of Mars. According to the tale, the twins, who had been raised by a she-wolf, competed for the right to rule. Ultimately, both claimed to have received the blessings of the gods. The disagreement over who would rule ended violently when Romulus killed his brother and became the sole ruler and founder of Rome. The important role of the prophet and the brothers' reliance on divinations to predict the future speak to ancient Roman tradition.

By 509 BC, Roman peoples wrested power from the last king and drove him out. They replaced the monarchy with the Republic, a government representative of the wealthy noble class of patricians. Underrepresented by and resentful of this patrician government, the masses of plebeians struggled for several centuries to gain political power. **"The Plebeians Fight Back"** highlights this struggle and some of the progress the plebeians made by uniting and pressuring the patricians. Legal achievements such as the laws of the Twelve Tables offered plebeians access to justice and protection from the wealthier class. By 287, the two classes had achieved a superficial equality including a plebeian-run assembly and seats in the Senate, but the real power still belonged to the patricians.

As class conflicts flared internally, outside powers posed political threats that Rome had to face as well. **"The Punic Wars"** describes the three wars in which the mighty Phoenician state of Carthage finally succumbed to Roman military strategy and strength. Rome won these wars both because of its support from loyal allies and its well-trained and organized army that consistently improved on Greek military strategy. With the Carthaginian power base eliminated and the later defeats of Macedonia, Greece, and Asia Minor, Rome could acquire vast territories all around the Mediterranean.

Unfortunately, all the military expansion as well as the long Punic Wars had wreaked havoc on Rome's agriculture and economy. More than anything else, the masses wanted a strong leader who would provide stability and help them meet their basic needs. They found this leader in Caesar, who passed laws to reestablish farms, expanded citizenship and trade among people in the Italian peninsula, and organized a new calendar. The final play, **"Hail Caesar,"** highlights this leader's popularity and his unprecedented power—an issue that worried wealthy senators enough to murder Caesar in 46 BC, the same year he was pronounced dictator. Unfortunately for the conspirators, Caesar's popularity only grew. Civil war broke out until his adopted son, Octavian, avenged Caesar's death, defeated his competitors, and came to power as the Emperor Augustus, ushering in an era of peace called the Pax Romana.

# ROMULUS AND REMUS

## CHARACTERS

**Kate  Gina  Amulius  Faustulus  Romulus  Remus  Numitor**

*Scene 1: Present-day Rome*

**KATE:** Hey, wait just a minute! This guidebook says that Rome was founded by twins who were raised by a *wolf*?

**GINA:** Sure, Romulus and Remus. A long time ago, maybe around 800 BC, there was a king named Numitor, but he had a brother, Amulius, who was jealous of his power. Numitor had a daughter named Rhea Silvia, and the god Mars fell in love with her—

**KATE:** The god Mars? The god of war? So this isn't a true story?

**GINA:** No, it's a legend. But it's a good story. So Rhea Silvia had twin boys, Romulus and Remus. Amulius found out and threw Rhea Silvia and her babies into the Tiber River. But the gods saved the babies. They sent a she-wolf who'd lost her own pups to raise the twins. Later, a shepherd named Faustulus found the twins . . .

*Scene 2: Sometime in the 8th century BC, near present-day Rome*

**NUMITOR:** Speak up, shepherd. What do you want?

**FAUSTULUS:** I was tending my flock, and I stumbled on twin boys—twin boys being raised by a wolf! I'm not kidding! Look, here they are! Romulus and Remus—your grandsons!

**NUMITOR:** How can this be? They were drowned in the Tiber!

**FAUSTULUS:** The gods must have been watching over them. They *are* half immortal.

**NUMITOR:** My grandsons! My daughter Rhea Silvia's sons! I'll make Amulius pay for keeping them from me.

*Scene 3: A few years later*

**ROMULUS:** Amulius is dead! At long last Amulius is dead.

**REMUS:** Let's build a city to celebrate. Let's build it on top of Aventine. That's my favorite hill.

Scholastic Professional Books, 2000

**ROMULUS:** You must be joking. Palatine is a much better hill for a city.

**REMUS:** You're wrong, as usual. Aventine.

**ROMULUS:** And you're being stubborn, as usual. Palatine.

**REMUS:** Aventine.

**ROMULUS:** Okay, I've got an idea. We'll let the gods decide.

**REMUS:** Look! You can see for yourself! Six vultures just flew over me!

**ROMULUS:** But look yourself! I count 12 vultures circling me! The city belongs on Palatine, and I'll be king.

**REMUS:** That's what you think!

*Scene 4: A few months later. Romulus plows a line around his city in preparation for building a wall.*

**REMUS:** You think a wall will keep out your enemies, brother? They'll jump over it just like this!

*(Remus jumps over the line.)*

**ROMULUS:** Then I'll kill them.

*Scene 5: Present-day Rome*

**KATE:** Well, go on. What happened?

**GINA:** Romulus killed his brother. He named the city Rome after himself. People said that the 12 vultures that flew over Romulus meant that the power of Rome would last for 1,200 years.

**KATE:** That's a pretty good story, but who really founded Rome, and when?

**GINA:** Nobody knows for sure. The Romans didn't write anything down for a long time. The real story got mixed up with legends along the line.

**KATE:** Well, I'm glad *somebody* founded Rome. I'm having a great time. How about a *gelato*?

# "ROMULUS AND REMUS"

## DISCUSSION QUESTIONS

• What does this founding myth reveal about the ancient Romans?
• Why do you think ancient Romans assigned the god Mars as the father of Romulus and Remus?

## ACTIVITIES

### THANKS TO THE ETRUSCANS AND GREEKS . . .

Offer students a blank map of Italy on which to color and label areas populated by Greeks and Etruscans during the reign of kings in Rome (753–509 BC). Direct students to add symbols and short captions to describe some of the contributions each group made to Roman culture. The finished maps should detail important geographical and cultural links to the development of Rome.

### CHANGING GOVERNMENTS

Challenge students to contrast the different forms of government in early Rome. On large sheets of craft paper, pairs or groups of students create a three-column chart with the following categories: Monarchy, Republic, and Empire. Ask students to develop symbols that represent important positions and show how people were organized under each form of government. For example, in the Republic category, two triangles side by side might represent consuls, while a huge circle around the number 300 just to the side and below it might represent the larger but less powerful Senate.

### WHOSE VALUES?

Conduct a class discussion about what the myth of Romulus and Remus reveals about Roman values. Record student ideas about social structure, politics, religion, and so on and post them on a chart. As students continue to study Rome, as a republic and as an empire, consult the list and have students compare their original predictions with their new understandings. Encourage students to change original predictions and add new values to the list. When opposing values arise, such as *a strong central leader* and *representative government*, advise students to organize separate value lists for different social classes.

## RESOURCES

### BOOKS

*Ancient Rome (Eyewitness)* by Simon James (Knopf, 1990)
*Ancient Rome* by Judith Simpson (Discoveries Library/Time-Life, 1997)
*How We Know About the Romans* by Louise James (Peter Bedrick, 1997)

# THE PLEBEIANS FIGHT BACK

### CHARACTERS

**Livia    Servius    Marcus    Plebeians 1–5    Octavia**

*Scene 1: Rome, 494 BC*

**LIVIA:** But why should plebeians have any voice in our republic? We patricians are better equipped to make decisions for them. We're rich; they're poor. That's the way it is. That's the way it'll always be.

**SERVIUS:** True, so true, my dear, but there are always troublemakers. They're happy enough to come to us whenever they need money.

**LIVIA:** Yes, but what happens when they don't pay us back? I don't enjoy putting someone into debt bondage, but really, what else can we do but let them pay us back by working for us? If a plebe can't even pay us back, how can he expect to run the republic?

**SERVIUS:** I tell you, my dear, I don't know who's more dangerous to Rome—one man who wants to be king and take power from us patricians, or the thousands of plebeians who want our power.

**LIVIA:** What is that racket outside? Servius, do go out and see what the fuss is all about.

*(Servius goes out. He quickly returns.)*

**SERVIUS:** It's the plebes! They've gone on strike!

*Scene 2: On a hill outside Rome that same day, the plebeian Marcus addresses a large crowd.*

**MARCUS:** The patricians want us to fight for Rome! And we have! We're proud Romans! We pay our taxes! We fight our fights! I came back from war and found my farm burned to the ground! My cattle were gone! I came to the city, but there's no work here for a free man! So a free man has to go into debt to the patricians to live. And then he's not a free man anymore!

**PLEBIANS 1–5:** You tell 'em, Marcus! No more workers! No more soldiers! No more taxes! We want freedom! We want freedom!

**MARCUS:** What do we want? Freedom! What do we demand? A voice in the republic!

*Scene 3: A few days later in Rome*

**SERVIUS:** We've discussed it in the Senate, and here's what we're willing to do: We'll cancel all debts and release any plebeians who've been imprisoned for debt.

**MARCUS:** It's a start. Now, what about plebian participation in the republic?

**SERVIUS:** *(Sighing)* Oh, very well. You can set up your own assembly—all plebeians, no patricians. You'll be represented by ten tribunes. You'll get to vote for them. Your tribunes can veto any action of the Senate, which will be all patricians, no plebeians.

**MARCUS:** As I said, it's a start.

*Scene 4: Rome, 451 BC*

**LIVIA:** What do they want *now*?

**SERVIUS:** The plebeians want the laws written down. They claim patrician judges are unfair to them.

**LIVIA:** Will it never end, Servius? Before you know it, plebeians will be allowed to marry patricians. And then where will we be?

**SERVIUS:** So true, Livia, so very true. But the laws are being written down right now, on bronze plaques.

*Scene 5: Rome, 442 BC*

**OCTAVIA:** It's perfectly legal now, Mother. I don't know why you're so upset.

**LIVIA:** Because he's a *plebeian*! You want to marry a *plebeian*!

**OCTAVIA:** He's Marcus' son. You like Marcus.

**LIVIA:** He's a plebeian. It doesn't matter whether I like him or not. Think of the lives your children will have to lead.

**OCTAVIA:** They'll grow up to be good, strong, brave, smart Romans—just like their grandparents are.

**LIVIA:** If we keep giving rights to the plebeians, then there won't be a Rome for your children when they grow up.

**OCTAVIA:** Of course there will, and I'm looking forward to the day when my daughter will be able to serve in the Senate.

**LIVIA:** A woman in the Senate!?! I need to sit down. You're giving me a headache.

# "THE PLEBEIANS FIGHT BACK"

## DISCUSSION QUESTIONS

- What did the plebeians gain from the patricians? What did the patricians gain from the plebeians?
- Why do you think it would have been difficult for the plebeians to abandon the patricians and form their own government somewhere else?

## ACTIVITIES

### A FAIR SAY

Invite a discussion based on the following question: *Do you agree that even without monetary power or family privilege, the plebeians still should have enjoyed representation equal to the patricians in the government of the Roman Republic?* Ask students for their opinions and help them draw comparisons to current examples of working-class people in various countries who may be struggling for a voice in government. What kinds of strategies do working-class people use to put pressure on government to change policies?

### CRIME, PUNISHMENT, AND SOCIAL STATUS

Ask students: *If you were an ancient Roman being tried for a crime, would you rather be in the position of a slave, a plebeian, or a wealthy citizen?* Compare the way punishments were meted out to different classes for the same crimes under Roman law with punishments under earlier Babylonian law (Hammurabi's Code). After students have researched the laws and drawn comparisons, have them synthesize the information by offering theories about why the two civilizations operated with such different expectations of their social classes.

### NEW HOPE FOR PLEBEIANS: THE GRACCHUS BROTHERS

During the years of heavy unemployment and agricultural devastation following the Punic Wars, two famous plebeian brothers, Tiberius and Gaius Gracchus, rose to positions of power (both as tribune) and passed reforms to help their people. Challenge students to write a dialogue about one of the Gracchus brothers between either two patricians or two plebeians. The dialogue should show the threat or promise that the tribune offers the Republic, addressing specific reforms proposed by the Gracchus brother chosen as the topic.

## RESOURCES

### BOOKS

*Ancient Romans: Expanding the Classical Tradition* by Rosalie F. and Charles F. Baker III (Oxford University Press, 1998)

*City: A Story of Roman Planning and Construction* by David MacAulay (Houghton Mifflin, 1983)

*Rome (The Ancient World)* by Sean Sheehan and Pat Levy (Steck-Vaughn, 1999)

# THE PUNIC WARS

## CHARACTERS

**Narrators 1 and 2     Roman Generals 1 and 2     Roman Engineer**
**Hamilcar Barca     Hannibal     Soldier     Cato     Scipio Aemilianus**

**NARRATOR 1:** Imagine two cities fighting three—three!—wars with each other for more than 100 years. That's what Rome and the Phoenician city of Carthage did, from 218 BC to 146 BC. These wars are known as the Punic Wars. *Punic* means "Phoenician" in Latin.

**NARRATOR 2:** It all started on the island of Sicily when the city of Messina was attacked by a gang of soldiers. The city asked both Carthage and Rome for help. Armies from both cities showed up, but then they started fighting each other.

**ROMAN GENERAL 1:** Carthage controls the Mediterranean Sea. But we Romans never give up. We've added more than a hundred warships to our navy.

**ROMAN ENGINEER:** Take a look at this, General.

**ROMAN GENRAL 1:** What is it?

**ROMAN ENGINEER:** A secret weapon. I call it the "crow." It goes on the front of a warship. The ship pulls up to an enemy vessel, the crow comes down. The spike on the end punches a hole in the deck, and then our sailors climb across the crow to the enemy ship!

**ROMAN GENERAL 1:** Brilliant! Hamilcar Barca and his Carthaginians won't know what hit them! The "Man of Lightning" is going to get struck down!

**NARRATOR 1:** The crow helped the Romans defeat the Carthaginians. After the first war, Hamilcar moved his army to Spain and began to build trade there. Because it had gained control of the Mediterranean trade, Rome grew rich.

**NARRATOR 2:** Hamilcar Barca hadn't forgotten about Rome, though. He made his feelings clear to his young son, Hannibal.

**HAMILCAR:** I want you to promise me, son, promise me you'll never accept friendship with the Romans.

**HANNIBAL:** I will use fire and steel to stop Rome, Father.

**NARRATOR 1:** Later, when Hamilcar Barca drowned, Hannibal took charge of the Carthaginian army in Spain.

Scholastic Professional Books, 2000

**NARRATOR 2:** And Hannibal came up with a bold plan.

**SOLDIER:** The Roman Senate is making plans to invade Carthage!

**HANNIBAL:** We won't wait for the Romans to come to us. We're going to Rome.

**SOLDIER:** But Rome controls the sea—

**HANNIBAL:** We're not going by sea. We're going over the Pyrenees Mountains, across the Rhone River, and over the Alps into Italy.

**SOLDIER:** But those mountains are high and cold and icy and—

**HANNIBAL:** They're not as cold and icy as the steel of a Roman sword. Get the elephants ready. Move!

**NARRATOR 1:** Although Hannibal lost many men and animals, it was a daring move. He arrived in Italy. The Roman general Quintus Fabius Maximus tried to slow down Hannibal by following the Carthaginian army and harassing it.

**NARRATOR 2:** The harassment made it harder for Hannibal's troops to get supplies. Today this military tactic is called "fabian," after Fabius Maximus. Then Romans and Carthaginians met in a huge battle at Cannae.

**HANNIBAL:** Steady, men. Keep the line long and thin. Let them come to us.

**ROMAN GENERAL 1:** Romans! There he is in the middle of the line! Charge! Down with Hannibal!

**ROMAN GENERAL 2:** They're giving way! Hannibal's retreating! Wait! What's going on? . . . No!

**NARRATOR 1:** Hannibal trapped about 50,000 Roman soldiers by pretending to retreat. Then his cavalry, which was on either side, closed in on the Romans.

**NARRATOR 2:** But the Romans didn't give up. They sent Scipio Africanus to fight in Carthage. Hannibal returned home with his troops and met Scipio near Zama. Scipio won. There were 50 years of peace until Roman leaders decided that Carthage should be destroyed.

**CATO:** Carthage has made herself strong again through commerce. We'll send Scipio Africanus' grandson to destroy Carthage for good!

**NARRATOR 1:** And so the third Punic war began.

**NARRATOR 2:** For two years, Roman soldiers attacked Carthage. Finally, they were successful.

**SCIPIO AEMILIANUS:** Tear down every house! Salt the fields! No one will ever live here again! Nothing will ever grow here again!

# "THE PUNIC WARS"

## DISCUSSION QUESTIONS

- What effect has technology had on waging war since ancient Roman times? Consider moving troops, designing weapons, and speed of communications.
- Why was it so important for Rome to defeat Carthage completely? How do you think history might have changed if the Carthaginians rather than the Romans had won?

## ACTIVITIES

### REPORTS OF THE WAR
Ask students to imagine themselves in the role of a Roman army messenger who delivers news of each battle back to the Roman Senate. Have students individually or in groups prepare oral reports about key battles to deliver to the class. Reports might include the location and duration of a battle; strategies, special weapons, and resources used by each side; and casualties sustained. Organize the presentation of reports chronologically to help students construct events and developments sequentially.

### MAPPING MILITARY MOVES
To supplement or provide an alternative to the oral report activity above, encourage students to develop military maps that either show strategic positions in a single battle (e.g., Hannibal's retreat strategy at Cannae) or trace routes taken by the armies to important battles of the Punic Wars. These maps can lend visual support to the oral presentations.

### WAR REPERCUSSIONS: ROME
Territorial acquisition, foreign resources, money, and power were some of the positive effects of the Punic Wars on Rome. But not every Roman citizen benefited. A class-constructed cause-and-effect chart can help students understand the devastating impact of war on the lower classes of Rome. A web organizer with "Punic Wars" at the center and effect bubbles radiating out from it works well. Encourage students to contribute ideas for effects in the areas of the economy, social structure, political reform, and agriculture. Such an organizer can help prepare students to understand why the lower classes may have supported a dictatorship and not a republican government.

## RESOURCES

### BOOKS
*Ancient Weapons and Warfare (Exploring History)* by Will Fowler (Lorenz Books, 1999)
*The Roman Fort (The Roman World)* by Peter Connolly (Oxford University Press, 1998)

### WEBSITES
Victori: The Roman Military (http://library.advanced.org/21665 )
   This 1998 ThinkQuest project site provides information about military tactics, weaponry, the Punic Wars, and resources.
The Glory That Was Rome (http://www.danshistory.com/rome.html)
   Select "Wars" for details on the battles of Cannae and Zama.

# HAIL CAESAR!

## CHARACTERS
**William Shakespeare    Julius Caesar    Calpurnia**
**Brutus    Cassius    Soothsayer**

**SHAKESPEARE:** They've almost finished building the Globe Theatre. I need to write a play for the new theater. Let's see . . . a comedy or a drama? A drama, I think . . . based on Julius Caesar. The greatest Roman emperor—

**CAESAR:** Not emperor. I was *not* a king. When Mark Antony tried to put a crown on my head, I refused it. I made myself a dictator. I had to. The republic had turned rotten.

**CALPURNIA:** My husband, Caesar, saved the Roman Empire. You'd better show just what kind of men murdered him, Will Shakespeare. Especially Brutus, one of Caesar's best friends.

**CAESAR:** I helped the poor. I gave them land in Roman colonies. I drained marshland so they could farm. I invented the Julian calendar. I—

**SHAKESPEARE:** Wait a minute. You're characters in *my* play. I know you were real, but you've both been dead for more than 1,600 years.

**BRUTUS:** Excuse me, but nobody understands what a hard choice I had to make. I had to sacrifice my best friend to make life better for hundreds of thousands of other Romans. Caesar was determined to end the republic and rule the Empire all by himself.

**CASSIUS:** Caesar changed the name of the month Quintilis to July—after himself. Julius, July—get it? He made himself dictator for life—for *life*. He would only work if he was sitting on his throne—his *gold and ivory throne*. They started dedicating temples to Caesar—as a *god*. Well, let me tell you, he was a *man*—a mean and greedy man. He didn't care about the Roman Empire.

**CALPURNIA:** Traitor! You're the mean and greedy one! And jealous, too!

**SHAKESPEARE:** Everybody better calm down, or I'm not going to write this play. I'll write about Hannibal or Alexander the Great instead.

**CAESAR, CALPURNIA, BRUTUS, CASSIUS:** No! No! Write about us!

**SHAKESPEARE:** All right, then. That's better. Now, as I recall, Caesar fired his bodyguards—

**CASSIUS:** He knew his life was in danger. He was just showing off, pretending to be tough.

**SHAKESPEARE:** As I was saying, Caesar fired his bodyguards and then went to the Senate in the middle of March in the year 44 BC.

**SOOTHSAYER:** Beware the Ides of March! (*I told him. I tried to warn him. Would he listen to me? Nooooo.*)

**CAESAR:** I didn't think my best friend, and the *wise* men of the Senate, were going to murder me.

**CALPURNIA:** Sixty of them! Sixty senators set upon him! Cowards! Not one of them went up to Caesar, man to man, face to face, to tell him what they thought was wrong.

**CAESAR:** Say, Will, I'm a writer, too. I wrote about my battles in Gaul.

**SHAKESPEARE:** We call it France today.

**CAESAR:** Huh, no kidding? I invaded Britain twice, too, you know. I was in Greece and Italy and Egypt, Asia Minor.

**SHAKESPEARE:** Unfortunately, I don't read Latin, but I hear your accounts are very good.

**CALPURNIA:** They stabbed him 23 times. Don't forget to put that in your play. Twenty-three times! Then they went rushing into the streets shouting, "Liberty!"

**BRUTUS:** I didn't. I was heartbroken.

**CASSIUS:** (*Rolling his eyes*) Here we go again.

**SOOTHSAYER:** Beware the Ides of March!

**CAESAR:** Heartbroken? Hah! You were heartbroken because your cowardly plan didn't work. My nephew Octavian took over Rome. For 200 years, with the Caesars ruling, there was peace.

**SHAKESPEARE:** The Pax Romana, I know. (*Clapping his hands*) Okay, everybody out! I've got a play to write.

**BRUTUS:** Be sure to show how much I thought about my decision—how hard it was for me.

**SHAKESPEARE:** OUT!

(*Everyone except Shakespeare leaves. He picks up his pen and begins to write.*)

# "HAIL CAESAR!"

## DISCUSSION QUESTIONS

- Do you agree with Brutus' reasoning for killing Caesar?
- Why was Caesar's reign and death a major turning point for Rome, which became an empire under the leadership of his heir, Octavian?

## ACTIVITIES

### CAESAR: DANGEROUS DICTATOR OR ENLIGHTENED LEADER?

What would a loyal Roman citizen have said to Brutus in defense of Caesar? Invite students to write a scene in which Brutus and the conspirators must explain to the people why they killed Caesar. To provide a literary link and historical contrast to the students' own scripts, select excerpts from Shakespeare's *Julius Caesar* for your playwrights to read aloud.

### THE PAX ROMANA AND EARLY CHRISTIANITY

The reign of Octavian ushered in an era of peace and prosperity for Rome, called the Pax Romana (27 BC–180 AD). During this time many religious beliefs and practices were tolerated by the Roman government and Christianity developed and began to spread through the Empire. Yet many Roman emperors perceived Christians as a serious threat and persecuted them, beginning with Nero in 64 AD. Invite students to study Roman policy toward religion in the Empire and open a discussion of why Roman emperors until Constantine responded to Christians this way.

### ANCIENT WOMEN: ROME AND GREECE

Pose the following questions to the class: *If you had to take the place of a woman in ancient Rome or ancient Greece, which culture would you select and why? Which culture allowed women more social, political, and economic freedom?* To extend this discussion, challenge pairs of students to read up on and then debate the roles of ancient women, with one partner defending the Greek perspective and the other taking the Roman side.

## RESOURCES

### BOOKS

*The Ancient City: Life in Classical Athens and Rome* by Peter Connolly and Hazel Dodge (Oxford University Press, 1998)

*Caesar and Rome* by Charlotte Bernard (Henry Holt, 1996)

*Julius Caesar (Cambridge School Shakespeare* series*)* edited by Tim Seward (Cambridge University Press, 1992)

### WEBSITE

De Imperatoribus Romains: An Online Encyclopedia of Roman Emperors (http://library.advanced.org/21665/enhanced/flinks.html)

# EXTENDING MINI-PLAYS:

# DRAMA AND PLAYWRITING IN YOUR CLASSROOM

### THEATER PLAY

Students will enjoy learning how to follow stage directions, adding gestures and facial expressions, and creating costumes and props. (See *Act It Out!*, page 92.)

### STUDENT-CREATED SCRIPTS

After students have performed several of the mini-plays, they will become familiar with their format and content. With this expertise and some guidance from you, they can attempt to write their own scripts using new historical material. Individual students, partners, or groups can write scripts that contribute to the class' study of history. Again, this activity may be carried out as a jigsaw: Groups of students focusing on different topics may write skits and perform them in chronological order, and they can also generate discussion questions to help their classmates think critically about the material. A quick reference on student scriptwriting follows. (See *Script Tips*, page 93.)

### FILL IN THE MISSING LINES

Before students attempt to create a whole script on their own, you may want to provide a scaffold to assist them. A skeleton script offers students a chance to develop key parts that are missing without starting from scratch. For example, you might delete all or a few of a character's lines to invite students to imagine appropriate responses, given the character's personality and motives and the historical situation. Stage directions may be left out as well. Having moved through this process once or twice, students may feel more capable of tackling an entire mini-play script on their own or in a group. (See *What's My Line? Practice Your Playwriting*, page 94.)

# ACT IT OUT!

Acting out your role gives you a chance to add a little personal flavor to the character you are playing, making your performance more enjoyable for your audience.

## KEEP THESE EXPERT ACTING HINTS IN MIND WHEN YOU ARE PERFORMING:

### 1. I HEAR YOU LOUD AND CLEAR

Pronounce each word very clearly and speak in a big voice. Your audience should be able to easily hear the lines you are speaking.

Try a couple of these tongue twisters to practice your ENUNCIATION:

  a) Sally sells seashells by the seashore.
  b) The linguini in Madagascar is great.

### 2. THE HANDS SAY IT ALL: USING GESTURES

Use gestures that fit what your character is saying. Gestures are hand, arm, and body movements that people use to add meaning to their words.

Try adding a gesture or two to bring these two sentences to life:

  a) I really don't know what you're talking about!
  b) Now, wait just a minute! You can't believe everything you hear!

### 3. TONE: SAY IT LIKE YOU MEAN IT

Change the tone of your voice to show your character's feelings. Making your voice sound sad, happy, angry, or surprised when you read a character's lines is another way to liven up your performance.

Try reading the following statements in the two different tones of voice listed for each:

  a) I really don't know what you're talking about! (angry or guilty)
  b) I can't believe it! I just can't believe it! (excited or upset)

# SCRIPT TIPS

*As you begin to write your own script, you'll need to think like a playwright. Here are some pointers about information that you must provide to those who will read and perform your script.*

## CAST OF CHARACTERS

Provide a list of the names of characters in your play. Under the title, list the characters in the order they appear in the script.

## SETTING

You must decide what the setting (the time and place) will be for your play. Write the setting as stage directions at the beginning of the play or include a narrator who describes the setting. Characters' lines may also give clues about where and when your play takes place.

 **STAGE DIRECTIONS**

Stage directions give hints to the actors about how the characters behave during the play. Use these brief notes to tell an actor how to say a line (e.g., *Angrily*) or how to move (e.g., *Raises fist*). Place stage directions in parentheses between the character's name prompt and the character's speech.

## DIALOGUE

Think creatively about what your characters will say and how they will respond to each other. Their dialogue makes up the majority of your script. Follow this format for writing dialogue: 1. the character's name followed by a colon (:) 2. any stage directions in parentheses and 3. the exact words the character should say.

> **JOE:** *(Exasperated)* Will you please help me with this?
> **ERIC:** *(Running over to Joe)* Of course! Why didn't you just ask?

Remember, it's up to you, the playwright, to help your audience understand what's going on. In your play, the dialogue has to explain everything, including thoughts, feelings, and background information.

# WHAT'S MY LINE?
## PRACTICE YOUR PLAYWRITING

**Directions:** In the mini-play below, some lines of dialogue are not complete. To finish the script, you must decide what the characters would MOST LIKELY say. The words must be historically accurate and fit into the dialogue sensibly.

**Hint:** Read through the entire script first. Then decide what to write for each missing section of dialogue.

## A ROMAN DINNER PARTY
### CHARACTERS
Narrator        Claudius Antonius: A Newly Elected Roman Senator
Maria: Antonius' Daughter        Peter: "Humble Class" Guest
Upper Class Guest        Vincenzo: Slave

**NARRATOR:** The guests arrive on time and are seated on the couches that surround the finely set table. It is a special dinner party to honor Claudius Antonius, who has just been accepted into the Roman Senate. That is the discussion as the slave, Vincenzo, serves the meal. This young slave and Antonius' daughter have become secret friends, however—a forbidden relationship. The "humble class" guest, Peter, sits at the table with the others but is not treated very well.

**CLAUDIUS:** Welcome to my dinner party, my noble guests! Well, all of you are noble, except for Peter, that is. *(Laughs)* Ah, Peter, how does it feel to dine with the upper classes? Of course, you will not eat all of the fine food that we do today. Still it is a privilege for you to dine with us.

**PETER:** *(Humbly)* _____

_____

**CLAUDIUS**: *(Sternly)* Slave! Where is the wine for our guests? Maria, help Vincenzo bring the wine to this table! Let us not be rude and allow our guests to go thirsty!

**MARIA:** Daddy, I can find only the expensive wine for our wealthy guests. Where is the

less expensive wine that we always give to _____

_____?

**CLAUDIUS:** *(Laughing)* _____

_____

**MARIA:** *(To Vincenzo, kindly)* Vincenzo, please do not serve Peter on the fine silver. He uses the pewter, like the servants do.

**VINCENZO:** *(Humbly)* _____

**GUEST:** *(Laughing)* Look at his clothes! So inferior! No man who wears such ridiculously cheap-looking clothing should eat and drink what the upper classes do. He doesn't even talk properly!

**CLAUDIUS:** Maria, help Vincenzo, please. It seems our good-for-nothing slave is not aware how to treat the different classes. Imagine serving poor Peter here on fine silver! Ridiculous!

**MARIA:** Yes, Father. *(To Vincenzo, quietly)* Do not be upset by my father's words. He is showing off for his guests.

**VINCENZO:** *(Without looking up)* _____

_____

**MARIA:** *(Kindly)* I understand how you must feel being treated this way. Let me help you.

**VINCENZO:** You are the only member of this house who is kind to me, Maria. Your father can be so cruel.

**MARIA:** _____

_____

**CLAUDIUS:** *(Loudly)* Maria, surely you are not conversing with this low-life slave? Let him do his work! You are a hostess and a member of the highest class of Rome. I will not have my daughter acting like a common servant, or worse, befriending the household slaves. Can you not read the sign on the wall over there? "Let the slaves wash and dry the feet of our guests." You are no slave! Come sit down at once, girl! Vincenzo should not even be speaking at all. One more word, you belligerent slave, and you will be flogged.

**MARIA:** *(Quietly to Vincenzo)* _____

_____

**CLAUDIUS:** Come everyone, a toast! Even Peter can raise his glass for this. A toast to your new senator and to many more gatherings with fine food and wine!

**GUEST:** _____

_____

_____

**NARRATOR:** As this dinner party clearly illustrates, the lines between the classes in ancient Rome were sharply drawn. There was no doubt in anyone's mind where everyone belonged in the social order of Rome.

# ADDITIONAL RESOURCES

**General Ancient History:**
*The Cartoon History of the Universe,
    Volumes 1-7* by Larry Gonick
    (Doubleday, 1990)
*A Message of Ancient Days* by Beverly
    Armento, Gary Nash, Christopher
    Salter, and Karen Wixson (Houghton
    Mifflin, 1991)
*Pockets World History* by Philip Wilkinson
    (Dorling Kindersley, 1996)
*Visual Factfinder: World History* by Ken
    Hills (Scholastic, 1993)

**Series:**
Steck-Vaughn *(The Ancient World)*
*Egypt* by Jane Shuter (1998)
*Great African Kingdoms* by Sean Sheehan
    (1999)
*Greece* by Robert Hull (1998)
*Rome* by Sean Sheehan and Pat Levy
    (1999)

Candlewick Press
*The Egyptian News* edited by Scott
    Steadman (1997)
*The Greek News* edited by Anton Powell
    and Philip Steele (1999)
*The Roman News* by Andrew Langley and
    Philip De Souza (1996)

Franklin Watts
*How Would You Survive as an Ancient
    Egyptian* by Jacqueline Morley (1996)
*How Would You Survive as an Ancient
    Greek* by Fiona MacDonald (1996)
*How Would You Survive as an Ancient
    Roman* by Anita Ganeri (1996)

Peter Bedrick
*How We Know About the Egyptians* by
    Louise James (1997)
*How We Know About the Greeks* by Louise
    James (1997)
*How We Know About the Romans* by
    Louise James (1997)

Scholastic
*Horrible Histories: The Awesome Egyptians* by
    Terry Deary and Peter Hepplewhite (1997)
*Horrible Histories: The Groovy Greeks* by Terry
    Deary (1997)
*Horrible Histories: The Rotten Romans* by Terry
    Deary (1997)

**China:**
*Ancient China* by Brian Williams (Penguin
    Group, 1996)

**Egypt:**
*Mummies Made in Egypt* by Aliki (Harper-
    Collins, 1979)
*Pharaohs and Mummies* by Anita Ganeri
    (Ladybird Books, 1996)

**Internet Sites:**
www.awesomelibrary.org/social.html
    Awesome Library teacher page for history
    site links.
www.fordham.edu/halsall/ancient/asbook.html
    Fordham University's Internet Ancient
    History Sourcebook (links to African, East
    Asian, Indian, and Jewish history sites).
www.wwlia.org/museum.htm
    The World Wide Legal Information
    Association's Law Museum Archives collec-
    tion (ancient laws and leaders).
www.wbonline.worldbook.com
    World Book Encyclopedia.